LUTHER'S TABLE TALK

A Critical Study

BY

PRESERVED SMITH

AMS PRESS
NEW YORK

COLUMBIA UNIVERSITY
STUDIES IN THE
SOCIAL SCIENCES
69

The series was formerly known as *Studies in History,
Economics and Public Law.*

Reprinted with the permission of Columbia University Press
From the edition of 1907, New York
First AMS EDITION published 1970
Manufactured in the United States of America

Library of Congress Catalog Number: 78-127457
International Standard Book Number:
   Complete Set . . . 0-404-51000-0
   Number 69 0-404-51069-8

AMS PRESS, INC.
New York, N.Y. 10003

PREFACE

THE following study aims to give a picture of the environment in which Luther and his guests conversed and of the men who noted down the sayings of the master. Each of these reporters was a source from whom others copied until practically all the sayings were united, after several stages of transcription, into great collections by various editors. We might compare the process of accumulation to that by which many springs pour their waters into the same great river, the original notebooks corresponding to the springs, the first copies to tributary streams, and the final editions to large rivers. From an account of this process, as little technical as possible, we naturally come to an appreciation of the literary and historical value of the Table Talk, treating it in a manner which is illustrative as well as critical.

Among many friends and scholars who have helped me with criticism and suggestion, I must thank especially those to whose constant interest I owe the most—Professor J. H. Robinson, Professor J. T. Shotwell, both of Columbia University, and my father, the Rev. H. P. Smith, D. D.

5

TABLE OF CONTENTS

7

CHAPTER I

LUTHER AND HIS GUESTS

IN the old town of Wittenberg the traveler may still see Luther's house looking much as it did three hundred and eighty years ago when he moved into it after his marriage. The veneration of posterity has restored it to the style of Luther's time and filled it with memorials of its famous occupant; pictures of Martin and Käthe on the walls; the old *cathedra* in the *aula* or lecture room; the bench on which Luther often used to sit with his wife, looking out on the neat garden in front.

The house had once been the Augustinian Monastery, and as such Luther's home for several years while he was a member of the order; but the progress of the reformed teaching had left it without occupants for some time before it became the dwelling of the ex-monk and his wife with their numerous dependents and guests. Here the reformer spent the happiest and most peaceful part of his career. The storm and stress of the previous years had given place to a period of comparative calm which was to last the rest of his life. The awful struggle in his own soul, the fierce revolt against the abuse of indulgences, the brave stand at Augsburg, the heroism of Worms, the imprisonment in the Wartburg and the perturbations of the Peasants' Revolt, all had passed. When Luther and his bride took possession of their home in June, 1525, they had before them twenty busy, useful years, years of comparative quiet and domestic happiness.

9

One cannot say years of domestic privacy. The Luthers kept open house and entertained not only their poor relatives such as old " Muhme Lehne " and their nieces, but many students as well, to say nothing of the distinguished strangers who visited Wittenberg. The table was always full. At the head the large form and strong face of the master would be conspicuous. He was a man of many moods, and his strong personality forced them on his guests, who took their cue from him, maintaining silence or talking seriously or jocosely as he set the example. At times he was lost in thought over some weighty problem of theology, or the vexatious attacks of the " Papists " or " Ranters," and again he was " happy in mind, joking with his friends." Near him we see the staid and dignified Schiefer, or the mournful Schlaginhaufen, intent upon his sins, or the irascible countenance of Cordatus. A strongly built woman, comely [1] in spite of her snub nose, serves the meal with the assistance of her female relatives, frequently participating in the conversation, occasionally the butt of an innocent joke from her husband, and sometimes quarreling with the students who kept Luther from his dinner with their interminable questions. Let us hear from one of those present what a meal was like at Luther's table: [2]

As our Doctor often took weighty and deep thoughts with him to table, sometimes during the whole meal he would maintain the silence of the cloister, so that no word was spoken ; nevertheless at suitable times he let himself be very merry, so that we were accustomed to call his sayings the con-

---

[1] Luther once thought her " wunderhübsch." Köstlin, *Martin Luther,* i, 764.

[2] Mathesius, *Luther Histories,* xii, 133a, quoted by Kroker, *Luthers Tischreden in der Mathesischen Sammlung,* Einleitung, p. 11. *Cf.* Köstlin, ii, 488, Anm. 1.

diments of the meal, which were pleasanter to us than all spices and delicate food.

If he wished to get us to speak he would make a beginning: What's the news? The first time we let the remark pass, but if he said again: Ye Prelates, what's the news in the land? then the old men would begin to talk. Doctor Wolf Severus [Schiefer] a travelled man of the world who had been the preceptor of his Roman Majesty's children, often was the first to introduce a subject, unless there was a stranger present.

If the conversation was animated, it was nevertheless conducted with decent propriety and courtesy, and the others would not take their turn at it until the Doctor spoke. Often good questions on the Bible would be propounded, which he solved finely, satisfactorily and concisely, and if any one took exception to any part, he would even suffer that and refute him with a proper answer. Often honorable people from the University were present, and then fine things were said and stories told.

Occasionally Luther would dictate something to one of the disciples. This was usually " some precious material in the interpretation of the Bible " such as the exegesis of the twenty-third Psalm which Rörer recorded one evening and had printed.[1]

Cordatus claims the honor of being the first to conceive

---

[1] Seckendorf, *Comment. Hist. de Lutherismo*, iii, 134. Seidemann, *Lauterbachs Tagebuch von 1538*, p. xiii. That this practice was common among the other disciples may be seen from Aurifaber's Introduction to his edition of the sermons: "These sermons have never been printed but by me, John Aurifaber, from the written books of honorable and blessed persons, such as M. Vitus Dietrich of Nürnberg, Item M. Georgius Rorarius, M. Antonius Lauterbach, and Herr Philip Fabricius (who took them from the holy mouth of Luther as he preached)." Quoted by Seidemann from the Eisleben edition of the *Sämmtliche Werke*, ii, 145b. These sermons were largely expositions of Scripture. *Cf.* also Seidemann, *ibid.*, p. 165; Bindseil's *Colloquia*, iii, 158.

the brilliant idea, so fruitful in later results, of taking down not only special pieces, but the general run of Luther's conversation.   At first he had some compunctions about the propriety of making notes at his host's table, but habit overcame them.   He says:

I was also aware that it was an audacious offence for me to write down everything I heard whenever I stood before the table or sat at it as a guest, but the advantage of the thing overcame my shame.   Moreover the Doctor never showed, even by a word, that what I did displeased him.   Nay more, I made the way for others, who dared to do the same thing, especially M. Vitus Dietrich and J. Turbicida [Schlaginhaufen] whose crumbs, as I hope, I shall join to mine, for the whole collection of pious sayings will be pleasing to me.[1]

The same reporter speaks of a notebook in which he kept the precious sayings, and Dietrich says that the notes were taken on the spot, just as if the disciples had been in the classroom.[2]   Still more explicitly Schlaginhaufen observes: " I took this down while we were eating, after a funeral." [3]

Little discrimination was shown by the students who sat around notebook in hand, eager to catch and transmit to posterity the gems which dropped from their master's lips, " which they esteemed more highly than the oracles of Apollo." [4]   Nothing was too trivial for them, and occasionally the humor of the situation would strike Luther.

---

[1] Wrampelmeyer, *Cordatus Tagebuch*, no. 133a.   The Latin at the end is incorrect, but this seems to be the sense; it is " M. Vitus Dietrich et J. Turbicida quorum micas (ut spero) illis meis conjunxero, omnis multitudo piorum gratis mihi erit."

[2] Dietrich, p. 165b.   " Sequuntur anno 1533 excerpta inter colloquendum."   Quoted by Preger, *Luthers Tischreden aus den Jahren 1531 und 1532 nach den Aufzeichnungen von Joh. Schlaginhaufen*, Einl., xiv.

[3] *Ibid.*, no. 465.

[4] Wrampelmeyer, *op. cit.*, Einl., p. 24, quoting Cordatus.

Once when a widower sent a messenger to Luther asking him for assistance in the selection of a wife, the master, after the departure of the messenger, turned to his disciple with a laugh, and said: "For Heaven's sake, Schlaginhaufen, put that down, too!" Schlaginhaufen himself records the incident.[1]

In this connection it naturally occurs to us to ask whether Luther really disliked the practice of notetaking or not. In spite of the assertion of Cordatus that Luther never showed even by a word that he was displeased with his disciples' assiduity, it is certain that at times he regretted it. He was aware that he was exhibited to the world in négligé. "In St. Augustine's books," he says, "one finds many words which flesh and blood have spoken, and I must confess that I speak many words which are not God's words, both when I preach and at table."[2] Again he was probably thinking of the Table Talk when he said:

I pray my pious thieves, for Christ's sake, not to let themselves lightly publish anything of mine (albeit I know they do it with an upright, loyal heart) either during my lifetime or after my death. . . . . I repeatedly pray them not to bear the burden and danger of such a work without my public consent.[3]

[1] Preger, *op. cit.*, no. 292.

[2] Hauspostille on the Gospel for the Sunday Jubilate. Walch: *Luthers Sämmtliche Werke*, xxi, p. 1248. *Cf.* also his preface to the "Little Sermons to a Friend," Walch, xii, p. 2375: "As we are men, there are many passages which are human and savor of the flesh. For when we are alone and dispute, we often get angry and God laughs at the extraordinary wisdom we display towards him. I believe he derives amusement from such fools as teach him how he should reign, as I often have done and still do." This preface to the *Conciunculae*, which appeared in 1537, was inserted by Cordatus as a preface to his Notes (Wrampelmeyer, Einl., p. 41). It may have been that Cordatus was the friend to whom it was addressed.

[3] Walch, *Conciones quaedam D. Mart. Luth.*, xx, 2373.

At times he complained specifically and bitterly of conversations published by his friends; but he never seems to have interfered with any one during the many years in which a large number of men wrote down his sayings in his presence.

Melanchthon, however, on one occasion rebuked the indiscriminate zeal of Cordatus. The reprimand is recorded by the disciple on whom it apparently had not the slightest effect. He tells the story as follows:

I wrote in my notebook these words: Luther to Melanchthon: "Thou art an orator in writing but not in speaking." For the candor of both the speaker and the listener pleased me. Melanchthon wished to persuade him not to answer a book edited by the pastor of Cologne, whom Luther calls Meuchler von Trasen. But what I wrote did not please Philip, and so when he had asked again and again for my notebook, wherein I was accustomed to write what I heard, at length I gave it to him, and when he had read a little in it he wrote this couplet:

> Omnia non prodest, Cordate, inscribere chartis,
> Sed quaedam tacitum dissimulare decet.

With quite unconscious humor Cordatus adds in the next section that he was confounded by Philip's poetry.[2]

---

[1] *E. g.*, in the *Conciunculae* quoted above, where he complains bitterly that his friends have published *sermones quos ipsum sub coena et prandiis effudisse* during his illness at Schmalkald.

[2] Wrampelmeyer, *op. cit.*, no. 133. The Latin, as generally in Cordatus, is confused, but the point is perfectly clear.

CHAPTER II

The Earlier Reporters of the Table Talk

LUTHER's life may naturally be divided into two periods by his marriage in June, 1525. Each period has its own character, sharply marked off from the other, and each has much internal unity. Nine-tenths of his political activity fell within the first period; it was a constant and fierce struggle; and by the time it was over the victory had been won and the great revolt from Rome was well under way. The second period was one of comparative quiet, of domestic experience, hospitality, preaching, teaching and writing; not less interesting than the more active part of Luther's career, but interesting in a different way. It is not so much the operation of a great political force as the significance of a great man's private life which now engages our attention.

With the exception of a doubtful note or two of Cordatus, all the records we have of the Table Talk fall within the second period. During these twenty years no less than a dozen men followed the practice of reporting their hero's words as he spoke them at table.[1] A list of these men at

---

[1] We know who took notes partly from the extant records, partly from references, especially the lists of their sources given by two collectors of Table Talk, Mathesius (*Luther Histories*, xii, 131b, quoted by Kroker, *op. cit.*, Einl., p. 13) and Aurifaber (preface to his printed edition, reprinted by Walch, *op. cit.*, xxii, 40-55). These lists give the names of three men who did not take notes: Rörer (Förstemann-Bindseil, *Deutsche Tischreden*, vol. iv, p. xvi; Lösche, *Analecta Lutherana*, p. 10), Ferdinand a Maugis (Seidemann, *op. cit.*, Einl., p. xii; Köstlin, *op. cit.*, ii, 618), and Weber (Kroker, *op. cit.*, Einl., p. 15). Besides the

this point will greatly clarify our subsequent discussion, especially if we put opposite the name of each the dates within which his notes were taken.

1. Conrad Cordatus. 1524-1537.[1]
2. Veit Dietrich (Theodoricus). 1529-1535.
3. Johan Schlaginhaufen (or Schlainhauffen, *alias* Turbicida, *alias* Ochloplectes, *alias* Typtochlios). 1531-1532.
4. Anton Lauterbach. 1531-1539.[1]
5. Hieronymus Weller. 1527-1538.
6. Antonius Corvinus. 1532.
7. Johannes Mathesius. 1540.
8. Kaspar Heydenreich (variously spelled). 1541-1543.
9. Hieronymus Besold. 1541-1546.
10. Magister Plato. 1540-1541.
11. Johannes Stolz (Stolsius). 1542-1546.
12. Johannes Aurifaber (Goldschmidt). 1545-1546.[2]

men mentioned in Mathesius' and Aurifaber's lists, we know that Cordatus (whose notebook is extant) took notes and that Corvinus probably did (Preger, *op. cit.*, no. 342). Others who have sometimes been thought to have taken notes, but who did not, are: Mörlin (Förstemann-Bindseil, *op. cit.*, vol. iv, p. xix; Kroker, *op. cit., Einl.*, p. 15), Schiefer (Lingke, *Merkwürdige Reisegeschichte Luthers*, 1769, Einl., p. 3; Seidemann, *op. cit.*, Einl., p. xii; Lösche, *op. cit.*, p. 9), Jonas (Kawerau, *Briefe d. J. Jonas* in *Quellengesch. Sachsens*, vol. 15, p. 104; F. S. Keil, *Merkwürdige Lebensumstände Luthers*, pt. i, p. 161), and Melanchthon (*Corpus Reformatorum*, xx, 519-608; Lösche, *op. cit.*, pp. 18, 19; Kroker, *op. cit., Einl.*, pp. 34-37).

[1] A very few notes of Cordatus and Lauterbach can be assigned to dates later than those given opposite their names, taken on their visits to Wittenberg.

[2] The notes of Cordatus, Dietrich, Schlaginhaufen and Lauterbach are extant in something like their original form. The notes of Mathesius, Weller, Heydenreich, Besold and Plato are preserved (each notebook by itself) in the Mathesian collection. Corvinus is known only in one note copied by Schlaginhaufen. The notes of Stolz and Aurifaber have become indistinguishably merged in the collection of the latter.

The twelve men just enumerated fall into two distinct groups, the notes of six falling within the first fourteen years of the period and those of the others within the last six years. Cordatus and Lauterbach, to be sure, who are included in the first group, took notes on their visits to Wittenberg after 1540, but these sayings are few and unimportant. It is convenient to give a short account of the individual reporters of each group, in order to get a clear picture of the environment in which they worked.

The years 1525-39, within which the first group took notes, were active and important, though their importance has been overshadowed by the great events of the eight years immediately preceding. Every one who knows the name of Luther, knows of the 95 Theses and the Diet of Worms, and the translation of the Bible. Only second to these in Luther's fame stand the appearance before the Cardinal Legate at Augsburg, the burning of Pope Leo's Bull and the Canon Law, and the three great pamphlets of 1520. All of these [1] came before his marriage. We might compare Luther's career to that of a conqueror in which the events and labors just spoken of are the great battles by which a new country is subdued. The work which follows is less showy, but not less difficult; Luther's problem was no longer to conquer new territory, but to consolidate and organize what had been already won.

Thus we see his efforts in these years were chiefly absorbed in regulating and developing the church he had founded; and in protecting it first from the inroads of Zwingli and the Swiss, and then from the internal strife which threatened it with schism. The two Diets of Speyer, the Diet of Augsburg of 1530, the Articles of Marburg,

[1] The translation of the New Testament was done by 1522, and that of the Old Testament under way, though not completed till 1534.

the Religious Peace of Nuremberg, and the Wittenberg Concord mark successive stages of Luther's participation in the evolution of Protestantism. Towards the end of the period the bigamy of Philip of Hesse begins to weigh heavily upon him. His writings are no longer the trumpet calls to arms which we hear in the "Appeal to the Christian Nobility" and "The Babylonian Captivity," but the catechism and the hymns which did so much to put the services of the Church on a solid foundation. His domestic life, though disturbed by fear of the plague in 1527, was happy, and marked by the birth of several children.

The first of the reporters, Conrad Cordatus, was about seven years older than Luther, having been born at Weissenbach in Austria in 1476. After a number of years spent in wandering and studying theology in several places, during which he lost a lucrative ecclesiastical office in 1517 by joining the revolt against Rome, he finally came to Wittenberg in 1524, and spent a year with Luther. Returning home he was imprisoned on account of his religion for nine months, but escaped and returned to Wittenberg in 1526. From this time on he was practically a dependent of Luther's, who several times got him positions which he could not hold. The first of these was to teach in the new Academy founded by Duke Frederick II of Leignitz and Brieg. The venture was not a success, however, and when the Academy failed, Cordatus was again without occupa-

---

[1] A short biography is given by Wrampelmeyer, *op. cit.*, Einl. The sources for his life have been collected by Götze in *Jahresb. d. Altmärk. Vereins f. Gesch. u. Alterthumskunde*, vol. xiv, p. 57 *et seq.* (1861). His *Deutsch Postille* or Sermons preached at Niemergk, 1534, were published with a preface by Melanchthon in 1554. Kolde, *Anal. Luth.*, publishes some of his letters to Melanchthon. Much material is found in his Notebook of the *Tischreden. Cf.* Wrampelmeyer, *op. cit.*, no. 1536, &c.

tion, and, after a short visit to his home, returned to Wittenberg in 1528. In 1529 he was called to be second pastor at Zwickau; but a sharp altercation with the burgomaster and Council caused him to leave " that Babel " two years later. For ten or twelve months (after August, 1531) he was Luther's guest; then he obtained an inferior position at Niemergk which he filled till 1537, when his hot temper got him into trouble again.[1]

While at Niemergk he maintained constant intercourse with Wittenberg, and some of his notes prove that he was still Luther's guest at times.[2] In 1536 he got into a dispute with Melanchthon, whom he called, with characteristic violence, " a crab crawling on the cross." [3]

In 1537 he was called to Eisleben, and from that time on filled several positions at a distance from Wittenberg, until his death, soon after that of Luther, in 1546.

In reporting Luther's sayings he showed more zeal than judgment, writing down whatever came in his way, whether he heard it himself or learned it from some one else. He may have begun the practice as early as 1524, but he did not take many notes until 1532, when he spent a year with Luther between his pastorates at Zwickau and Niemergk. After his call to Niemergk in 1533 he made occasional visits to Wittenberg, during which he took some notes, closing the record in 1537, when he went to Eisleben.

His intimacy with Luther is proved by anecdotes of which the notebook is full. He affectionately relates that

---

[1] Wrampelmeyer, *op. cit.*, no. 1462. He complains of his hard life at Niemergk and Luther comforts him.

[2] These dates, however, are uncertain.

[3] Kolde, *Anal. Luth.*, p. 279. *Cf.* Köstlin, ii, 455. They were afterwards reconciled and Melanchthon edited his sermons.

Luther often offered him his silver goblets in case of need. Again when he and Hausmann were sitting with Luther, the master remarked that a gift of 200 gulden would not please him so much as their company.[1] The pair resembled each other in fearlessness and violence. Luther well characterized Cordatus (and unconsciously himself) when he said: " When God needs a legate who shall set forth his affairs strongly and dare to correct the vicious, he uses the wrath of some person like Cordatus, a man hard in speech and temper." [2] His irascibility must have made him at times an unpleasant guest. He was generally on bad terms with Käthe, and sometimes with his fellow guests. One day the conversation waxed so interesting that Luther forgot to eat. When Käthe tried to recall her husband to mundane affairs he replied with some warmth that she ought to say the Lord's prayer before she spoke. " Then I," demurely observes Cordatus, " tried to bring him back to the former subject of conversation by asking him about Campanus and his redundant style." [3]

When Luther, to his regret, could not help his friend Hausmann with a small loan, Cordatus had the bad grace to ask him why he had just let Käthe buy a garden, to which Luther replies, rather weakly, that he could not withstand her prayers and tears.[4]   Again Cordatus records a biting remark about Käthe's loquacity. " He called the long speeches of his wife ' a woman's sermons ' (*mulierum praedicationes*), because she would constantly interrupt his

[1] Wrampelmeyer, nos. 56 and 57. *Cf.* for other anecdotes nos. 989, 1408, 253, 133a.
[2] *Ibid.*, Einl., p. 13 *et seq.*
[3] *Ibid.*, nos. 111, 111a, 111b.
[4] *Ibid.*

best sayings. And Dr. Jonas has the same virtue [? of interrupting]." [1]

Occasionally Luther felt called upon to administer a mild rebuke, as when Cordatus asks for an explanation of the expression *concupiscentia oculorum*. Again Luther tells him plainly, " You wish to be master and perchance to be praised, and thus you are tempted." [2]

Cordatus was middle-aged before he knew Luther. Dietrich, on the other hand, was a mere youth when he first met him. Born at Nuremberg, 1506, he came to Wittenberg in 1522,[3] with the intention of studying medicine, a vocation which Luther [4] induced him to abandon for theology. In 1527 he became a sort of amanuensis to Luther, accompanying him in this capacity to Koburg in 1530, and thence to the Diet of Augsburg in the same year.[5] He lived at Luther's house from 1529 to 1534, leaving in this year partly, perhaps, on account of a quarrel with Käthe,[6] but also doubtless because he was contemplating marriage, which took place in the next year. He was called to the pastorate of St. Sebald, in Nuremberg, in May, 1535, by the Council of that city. In this position he still maintained close relations with Luther and Melanchthon. In 1537

---

[1] Wrampelmeyer, no. 120. Jonas reciprocated by calling him a firebrand. *Corpus Reformatorum*, iii, 1500.

[2] *Ibid.*, nos, 74, 75, 115, 116, 161, 162.

[3] This date is given by Kroker, Einl., p. 8. Herzog in *Allegmeine Deutsche Biographie* gives 1527. My account is taken partly from Herzog, partly from Köstlin, and partly from Kroker, who used the unpublished *Tagebuch* and corrected some errors in previous accounts. A Life by Storbel came out in 1772. His correspondence is in *Corpus Reformatorum*.

[4] Dietrich, fol. 186, quoted by Köstlin, ii, p. 200, note 1, "*vocatio qua me a medicina ad theologiam vocaverat.*"

[5] Köstlin, ii, 514, 523. Herzog is in error in *Allg. Deut. Bib.*

[6] *Cf.* Kroker, Einl., 8.

he subscribed to the Schmalkaldic Articles on behalf of his Church. Ten years later he attended the Colloquium at Regensburg.

Dietrich was drawn into several theological quarrels.[1] Like Cordatus, he was a quick-tempered man, and took any contradiction of his views much to heart. His last years were embittered by the triumph of his enemies and broken by ill-health. He died at Nuremberg in March, 1549.

He wrote little of his own, but was an active editor and translator of Luther's writings.[2] His own notes and the copies he made from those of others are extant either in their original form or in copious extracts.[3] They testify his constant attendance on his master. He nursed him through the severe illness which attacked Luther in 1530, after the Diet of Augsburg. If we may believe the man of God, this affliction was due to the direct interposition of the devil, whom he saw in the form of a fiery snake hanging from the roof of a neighboring tower. With his habitual shiftiness, however, the old Serpent changed his form into that of a star when Luther endeavored to point him out to his disciple.[4]

Johann Schlaginhaufen, a native of Neunberg in the Upper Palatinate, makes his first appearance in May, 1520, when he matriculated at Wittenberg.[5] He was ap-

---

[1] The first of these was on the question of private *vs.* general absolution, Osiander supporting the former and Dietrich the latter. The second was on the elevation of the Elements. The restoration of this practice at Nuremberg, 1549, broke his health.

[2] Herzog, *loc. cit. Cf.* Köstlin, ii, 157.

[3] His notes are not printed. Seidemann prepared them for the press and his copy was used by Köstlin. *Cf. infra.*

[4] Dietrich, fol. 143, quoted by Köstlin, ii, 206.

[5] G. Bossert, in *Ztschr. f. kirch. Wiss.*, 1887, p. 354 *et seq.* New material on his life added by Preger, Einl., p. vi.

parently slow of study, for the next time he emerges, eleven years later, he is still a student, and a table companion of Luther besides, as we know from his notes of 1531 and 1532. In the latter year he was employed at Zahna, a mile from Wittenberg, whence he kept up an intimate relation with his former host. Ill-health and poverty clouded his sojourn here, which was, however, short, as he was called in December, 1533, to the more promising field of Köthen, as pastor of St. Jacob. Prince Wolfgang of Anhalt-Köthen made him superintendent, but did not support him in the plan of church visitation he attempted to introduce. This complicated the situation, and being still troubled by ill-health and small means, he sought another position, and obtained, at Luther's recommendation, the pastorate of Wörlitz. Here his health improved, his compensation was more adequate, and his plans of church visitation and remodelling the service on that of Wittenberg worked smoothly and successfully.

With his friend Helt, Schlaginhaufen went to Schmalkalden in 1537 as a representative of his church, for which he subscribed to the Articles. He then went home with Luther, who was suffering terribly from the stone, from which he hardly expected to recover, but of which he was suddenly relieved at Tambach. The disciple carried the news of his master's recovery back to the Prince, who had stayed behind, and was so full of it that, as he galloped into the town, he shouted triumphantly to the Papal Nuncio, whom he saw looking out of a window, *Lutherus vivit!* [1]

The date of Schlaginhaufen's death, which must have been later than 1549,[2] is not precisely known. His authen-

---

[1] Köstlin, ii, 399, 400.

[2] As we know from a letter of Jonas to Chancellor Rabe, in Kawerau, *Briefwechsel d. J. Jonas*, ii, 287.

tic literary remains are confined to a sermon, in a rousing style, preserved in the archives at Zerbst, and a book of *Tischreden* which we possess in a copy possibly made by his son-in-law, J. Obendorfer of Köthen.[1]

Schlaginhaufen won a place in Luther's household by many a little service gladly performed in return for his entertainment, for which he was too poor to pay. It is pleasant to believe that he got along with Käthe and the children better than some of the other guests. When Luther fainted, at the election of Rector, May 1, 1532, Käthe sent the little girl to notify him first, and then Melanchthon and Jonas.[2]

The poor fellow was much troubled with melancholy, which took the form of unceasing lamentation over his sins. Luther, whose own early struggles had given him a fellow-feeling for his disciples, was wondrous kind and patient in comforting him. When Schlaginhaufen fainted on December 31, 1531, Luther indulged in a violent invective against the malice of Satan, and prescribed various methods of foiling him. When restored to a semi-conscious state, the victim of the diabolic machination could only groan out " My sins! my sins!" but a quarter of an hour more of exhortation and ghostly comfort finally enabled him to rise and go home.[3]

---

[1] Bossert attributes to him a witty satire on Eck, written 1530, entitled *Eckii Dedolati ad Caesaream Maiestatem Oratio*. (*Cf.* Pirckheimer's *Gehobelte Eck* or " Rounded-off Corner.") This was probably not his however, but by a writer with a similar name—Schlahinhaufen. *Cf.* Preger, Einl., vi *et seq.*

[2] Preger, no. 77. He obtained the degree of master at an unknown date. *Cf. ibid.*, no. 323.

[3] Seidemann, p. 57. *Cf.* Luther's letter to him Mar. 10, 1534, De Wette, *Luther's Briefe*, vi, 148, wrongly quoted by Preger as Mar. 10, 1532, De Wette, iv, 494.

We now come to Anton Lauterbach, the most copious of all the notetakers, as well as one of the most energetic of later editors. Born at Stolpen in 1502, of well-to-do parents, he matriculated at Leipzig in the summer-semester of 1517 as of the " Meissen " nation.[1] He came to Wittenberg in September, 1521,[2] for a short visit, but he did not become a regular student there until April, 1529. He gives us much the same testimony as Luther on the prevalent lack of Biblical teaching. " I was a bachelor before I ever heard any text from the Bible, which was a mighty scarce book in those days." [3] He took his master's degree at Wittenberg, and became a frequenter of Luther's table in 1531.

In 1533 Lauterbach was called to fill the office of deacon at Leisnig; but a quarrel with the pastor caused him to seek, and obtain, a similar position at Wittenberg.[4] Here he was married, in the same year, to a nun named Agnes, and probably lived with his father-in-law, at least for a while. He was, however ,a frequent guest at Luther's, if not a constant boarder for many years. During 1538, especially, he noted sayings of Luther for almost every day. He had similar *Tagebücher,* though not so full, for other years.

His regular connection with Luther was terminated in

[1] His father may have been the burgomaster of that name. My account is taken mostly from Seidemann, Einl., p. v *et seq.*—an elliptical series of references to authorities, with a few words thrown in here and there. Anton tells an interesting story of his father and Tetzel. Bindseil, iii, 248.

[2] If he is not mistaken in saying so; he may have confused the date, or 1521 may be a slip for 1541.

[3] Note in Bindseil, i, 136 (not in Dresden MS.).

[4] In 1536. See De Wette, iv, 583, 672; v, 37, with Kroker, Einl., 9 Anm.

July, 1539, when he himself was called to Pirna, an event which he relates in the following terms:

When Master Anthonius Lauterbach was called away by the Senator of Pirna, he bade adieu to his teachers, and asked that he might be kept as deacon still. Doctor M. Luther answered: " It seemed good to God to call thee to the pastorate of Pirna, and thou doest well that thou obeyest, and although we would willingly keep thee here, we may not act contrary to his will." [1]

He returned to Wittenberg once a year to see his old hero, and take down a few more of his precious words.[2] After a long and acceptable ministry in Pirna he died there in 1569.[3]

Lauterbach's hobby was recording, collecting and arranging Luther's sayings. Käthe's shrewd remark [4] that of all the disciples whom Luther taught gratis Lauterbach profited the most, was fully justified, at least if we may judge by the quantity of material which he has left us. He took notes himself pretty constantly from 1531-1539, and also on the short visits he later made to Wittenberg. Besides his own notes he made a large collection of the notes of his fellow-students. Finally he endeavored to blend all these sayings into one great collection, a piece of work which, in spite of repeated efforts, he could never complete to his own satisfaction. No less than four redactions of such a collection have come down to us, one of which was the basis of the famous edition of Aurifaber.[5]

[1] Bindseil, iii, 127.

[2] Proved by notes of his taken in these years.

[3] Seidemann, p. viii. His bust may be still seen over the sacristy.

[4] Kroker, no. 332.

[5] For his notebooks, see *infra*, chapter iv; for his collections, chapter v.

Hieronymus Weller was born at Freiberg in 1499. He studied twice at Wittenberg, the second time in 1525, when, under Luther's influence, he changed from Jurisprudence to Theology. In 1527 he came into Luther's house, where he lived until 1536, when his marriage with Anna am Steig necessitated his setting up housekeeping for himself. In May, 1538, he left Wittenberg to become court preacher to the Prince of Anhalt and Dessau; in 1539 he was called to his native place as Professor of Theology, in which situation he lived until his death in 1572.[1]

Weller is a less conspicuous and a less amiable figure than some of Luther's other guests. He took little part in the conversation, scarcely any of his remarks having been recorded. On one occasion he is " consoled " by Luther in a way somewhat disparaging to his character, and on another the company reflects rather severely on his cowardice.[2] His notes must have fallen between 1528 and 1537. A considerable number of them have come down to us,[3] but they are of little value, as they were taken in a slovenly way, and mixed at random with notes copied from others, especially from Lauterbach.

Antonius Corvinus is known to us only through one note which Schlaginhaufen says he copied from him.[4] It is an explanation of what the remission of sins is. If he really took notes, they were probably few, especially as he was never long at Wittenberg.

Born at Marburg, 1501,[5] he first appears to history as

---

[1] Kroker, Einl., 10.　　　　　　　[2] Seidemann, pp. 71, 141.

[3] At least if Kroker is right in identifying sections 4 and 8 of his publication with Weller's notes.

[4] Preger, no. 342.

[5] My account of Corvinus is taken partly from the *Allg. Deut. Bib.,* partly from Kroker, Einl., p. 11. Corvinus wrote an account of Eras-

a monk in the cloisters of Rigdagshausen and Loccum, where he probably obtained his education. The attraction of Luther's teaching brought him to Wittenberg for a short time in 1525. We see him in Marburg in 1526 as preacher and professor in the new University of that city. Later he became connected with Philip of Hesse, and took part in the Conventions of Ziegenhain (1532), Cassel (1535), where Melanchthon and Bucer had a disputation, and Schmalkalden (1537). He was active in propagating the Reformation beyond the borders of Hesse, for which the enemies of the new faith imprisoned him from 1549 to 1553. Shortly after his release, at the intercession of Duke Albert of Prussia, he died.

mus's attempt to reconcile the two Churches about 1533. It is described as " impartial and conciliatory," which is hard to believe when we learn that Luther wrote an introduction to it. Köstlin, ii, 320.

CHAPTER III

The Younger Group of Reporters

In spite of domestic sorrow and increasing ill-health, the last years of Luther's life show no relaxation of that indomitable spirit and energy which had characterized the vigor of his young manhood. Vexed by the bigamy of Philip, and the use made of it by the " Papists," and worried by the illness of Melanchthon in 1540, the religious conferences at Worms and Regensburg in 1541 and the measures necessary to discipline the Reformed Church made severe demands upon his strength in the following years. He found time, however, to revise his translation of the Bible, and to produce a number of polemic and homilectic works. His sufferings from the stone became constantly worse, and his feelings were harrowed, at first by the dangerous illness of his wife in 1540, and still more by the death of his favorite child, Magdalene, at the age of thirteen, in 1542. We find him as active as ever in the last year of his life, and only a few weeks before his death in February, 1546, he undertook a journey to Eisleben.

One by one all the young men who had been accustomed to take notes at his table left him, and for a while, at the end of 1539, there was a time when his conversations were not reported at all, which one would think would have been a great relief to him. Other students soon appeared, however, to renew the practice, and Lauterbach and Cordatus made occasional visits during which they would improve the convivial hour by collecting a few notes in their old way.

Luther probably entertained his students gratuitously.

There is never any mention of board bills in the Table Talk, and when Luther speaks of a financial transaction between a student and himself, the student is usually the beneficiary.[1] Doubtless some of them, as Dietrich, Lauterbach, and Aurifaber, paid for their entertainment in services as secretaries. The relation of *famulus* is one which has lasted to the present day, and is immortalized in the person of Faust's Wagner. Other students, as perhaps poor Schlaginhaufen, may have been taken for charity, and so expected to be ready to do odd jobs in return: possibly Cordatus would have been kept as a well-known theologian and sufferer for the Protestant cause. Luther's carelessness and generosity in money matters is well established; but he may have taken something from those of his guests who could afford it, rather however, in the way of gifts, than of stipulated rent or board.[2]

Of the younger group of reporters, Johannes Mathesius, who was to rival Lauterbach in the diligence with which he collected Luther's Table Talk, and to surpass him in the discrimination with which he arranged it, was first on the scene. His father was a Councilor of Rochlitz, where he was born in 1504.[3] Johann attended the so-called "trivial"

---

[1] As where he records having paid something to have a student's room done over. *Hausrechnung*, De Wette, *op. cit.*, vi, 328. This shows that Plato (the student in question) roomed as well as boarded with Luther.

[2] Köstlin, ii, 498 *et seq.*, gives a full account of Luther's means of support, chief of which was his salary from the Elector of 300 florins besides something "in kind." He also made a profit from his garden and brewery and received occasional gifts. The translator of Köstlin (Chas. Scribner & Sons), whose name is not given, says that Luther, like other professors, took boarders for pay. I am unable to find this in the original. Professor Calvin Thomas kindly informs me that it was unusual for poor students to pay; and it may be that the practice of entertaining them was a survival of the old monastic custom.

[3] His life, which I have consulted, was published by G. Lösche under

school, (i. e. school in which the elements or *Trivium* were taught), and, after 1521, the Latin school at Nuremberg. During the years 1523-1525 he studied at Ingolstadt, from whence he drifted into Bavaria, where he became converted to the Protestant cause. The renown of Luther and Melanchthon drew him to Wittenberg in 1529, but he did not, at this time, come into close relations with his teachers. In 1530 he was called as *Baccalaureus* to the school at Altenberg, and in 1532 was promoted to the headmastership of the Latin school at Joachimsthal, a mining town which had recently sprung up. Although his beneficent activity in this position drew many scholars and spread the fame of the school and its head, he had always felt a preference for the clerical calling, and when about thirty-five years old the opportunity came to him to follow his inclination. The providential means of fulfilling his pious wishes was a lucky speculation in mines [1] which by 1540 had enabled him to realize enough to re-enter Wittenberg as a theological student. The recommendations of Jonas and Rörer got him the much-prized honor of a seat at Luther's table.

Mathesius has been called, though incorrectly, Luther's *famulus*.[2] How long he was his guest is not certainly known, but probably no longer than from May to November, which is the period covered by his notes of the Table Talk. That he was still occasionally invited to Luther's

---

the title, *Johannes Mathesius. Ein Lebens- und Sittenbild aus der Reformationzeit* (last edition 1904). The same scholar published his *Ausgewählte Werke*, 4 Bd., Prag, 1904 (2d edition). Short lives of Mathesius are given in Kroker, Einl., p. 11 *et seq.*, and Lösche, *Anal.*, p. 7 *et seq.*

[1] He became a partner in the lucrative mining business of Matthes Sax in 1538.

[2] Lösche, *Anal.*, p. 7, n. 4; Kroker, p. 11 *et seq.*

table, we know from the fact that in the lectures he later gave on Luther's life, he sometimes relates anecdotes of his hero's conversations from the years 1541 and 1542.[1] The reason he had to leave the house in November was due to the circumstance that he had collected a number of pupils to tutor. At first Luther kindly took the pupils with the master, boarding as many as four at one time, but when Mathesius added still others he saw he had to draw the line somewhere and the promising boarding schol left the house to seek some less inspiring, if more expensive, refectory.[2]

After taking the degree of master in September, 1540, he spent nineteen months more in study, and then returned to Joachimsthal in the capacity of deacon. He visited Luther in the spring of 1545 and later became pastor of the church at Joachimsthal, where he died in October, 1565. During his later life he made a collection of *Tischreden* taken down by others, and added them to his own.

We have already seen in what enthusiastic terms he speaks of the privilege of eating with Luther, and hearing him converse.[3] His statement, made long afterwards in a sermon, that the disciples would not speak until spoken to, and that then it was usually Schiefer who answered for the company, is curiously borne out in his notes. He hardly ever mentions himself or any of the younger men as saying a word; the name of Schiefer however, appears often. We observe too, that a greater number of jokes are recorded in his notes than in any of the earlier notebooks, a pleasant proof that Luther was not weighed down

---

[1] The *Luther Histories*. Out of 32 pages, 26 are devoted to anecdotes of the year 1540, 4 to 1541, and 2 to 1542.

[2] Kroker, Einl., p. 40, quoting *Luth. Hist.*, xiv, 165b, and xvii, 209. See also Kroker, no. 167.

[3] *Supra*, p. 10.

by the cares of his declining years, and an incidental indication of the increasing reverence in which he was held. The first reporters had noted down only serious remarks, now facetious, even damaging ones, are considered worthy of record.[1]

He himself was less zealous in taking notes at first than he was afterwards, and occasionally missed a good chance, as we see in an anecdote in a sermon he preached many years later. He relates there that on Whitsuntide, 1540, he heard Luther recount the story of his life up to the Diet of Worms. Of this story, which impressed itself so deeply on his memory, there is nothing in the *Tischreden*.[2]

Kaspar Heydenreich, another of the reporters, was born in Freiberg, 1516. He was the successor of Mathesius in the headmastership at Joachimsthal in 1540, but resigned this position in 1541, and went to Wittenberg, where he took the degree of master on September 15 of the same year. On October 24, 1543, he was called to the position of court preacher to the Duchess Katharina, widow of Henry the Pious, whose residence was Freiberg. He followed her later to Torgau, where he became superintendent. Here he died in his seventieth year in 1586. A considerable number of his notes falling between 1541 and 1543 found their way later into the Mathesian collection.[3]

---

[1] For jokes, see Kroker, nos. 3, 27, 90, 94, 95, 96, 99, &c. We also see Luther's preoccupation with Philip's bigamy during this period. *Cf. ibid.*, nos. 181, 182, 188, 189, 200, 206, 210, &c.

[2] *Luther Histories*, xiii, 147a. (Quoted by Kroker.) It is possible, of course, that he may have been mistaken in the date.

[3] A short notice of his life is found in Kroker, Einl., p. 13. His authority is K. G. Dietmann: *Die gesamte der ungeänderten Augsp. Confession zugethane Priesterschaft in dem Churfürstenthum Sachsen.* Bd. 4, p. 738.

Hieronymus Besold was born at Nuremberg about 1520. He came to Wittenberg to study in 1537 and attached himself to Melanchthon with whom he soon became a favorite. He did not begin his notes until after 1540, however, and only a few of them, belonging to the year 1544, have survived, in the Mathesian Collection. He was still Luther's guest at the time of the Reformer's death, after which he went to board with Melanchthon. Through the recommendation of the latter, he obtained a position at Nuremberg in November, 1546. His career was checkered, due to his varying attitude on the Interim. In 1555 he took the opinion contrary to that of his father-in-law, Osiander, and signed the *Confessio Anti-Osiandrina*. In 1562 he was carried off by the plague.[1]

He completed the work, left unfinished by Dietrich's death, of editing the *Enarationes in Genesin*. His notes are of little value. It is painful to discover that he was, like Cordatus and Dietrich, on bad terms with Käthe, whom he considered a " domineering, avaricious woman," and of whom he stood in awe at first. Later their relations improved, and Käthe used him to perform some little household commissions, a willing return on his part, for the hospitality shown him.[2]

Of Master Plato, whom Mathesius speaks of as one who took notes after him, we know but little. He was probably Georgius Plato Hamburgensis who took his master's degree at Wittenberg, September, 1537. Luther speaks of paying five florins to renovate his room in 1542, which would indicate that he not only boarded but lodged with

---

[1] Förstemann-Bindseil, vol. iv, p. xiv; Kroker, Einl., p. 13. Only 19 sayings are attributed to him. (Kroker, nos. 260-271.)

[2] Köstlin, ii, 496.

his professor. His notes fall in 1540. He followed the bad practice which we discovered in Cordatus, of introducing the notes of others freely among his own, taking Mathesius especially as a source from whom to copy. We know his record in three copies, one that used by Melanchthon later in giving his lectures. Luther speaks of him as an ardent opponent of the Papacy.[1]

Johannes Stolz was a Wittenberger by birth. He was matriculated as a student at that university in the winter-semester of 1533-1534. In 1537 he went with Jacob Schenk to Freiburg, but soon returned. He took his master's degree at Wittenberg, September 18, 1539, and three days later was called to the pastorate at Jessen, but shortly after returned to Wittenberg as docent. In 1546 he was dean of the Philosophical Faculty. In 1548 he was court preacher at Weimar. He died late in 1558 or in 1559. His notes have become indistinguishably lost in the Aurifaber collection. They must have fallen between 1542 and 1546 when he was with Luther.[2]

Johannes Aurifaber, the last of the reporters, and the first and most famous of the editors of the *Tischreden*, was born in the county of Mansfeld, about 1519. In 1537 he was sent to Wittenberg by the help of Count Albrecht Michael. In 1542 he became tutor to the young count of Mansfeld, and a year later field chaplain for the same patron. In 1545 he again returned to Wittenberg and spent

[1] Kroker, 235. Plato is ignored by the *Realencyclopaedie* and the *Allg. Deut. Bib.* Mentioned only once by Köstlin, ii, p. 676 n. to p. 487. He refers to De Wette, vi, 328, "Luthers *Hausrechnung*," where we find the entry "5 *Platon Stublin.*" The note there calls him "Simon Plato Nobilis Pomeranus," but Kroker shows this to be incorrect and gives the true name. Einl., p. 14.

[2] This resumé is taken from Kroker, Einl., p. 14.

a year with Luther as his guest and *famulus*, accompanying him in the latter capacity to Eisleben in the last year of Luther's life. After his death, Aurifaber again became field chaplain in the army of the Elector of Saxony in the Schmalkaldic War, and in 1550 he was appointed court preacher to John Friedrich der Mittlere.[1] He took an active part, on the side of the Gnesiolutherans, in the quarrels which arose among the former leader's students. Employed in various diplomatic and confidential missions in the next few years, he got himself into trouble with Chancellor Brück on account of his firm stand against the sectaries. He was obliged to flee to Mansfeld in 1561, where his old patrons maintained him in leisure for some years. It was during this time that his *Tischreden* was prepared for publication (the book appeared in 1566) and others of his works relating to Luther. In 1565 he became pastor at Erfurt, and won the favor of the council there. He died ten years later in 1575.

In his first stay at Wittenberg, he did not come into personal contact with Luther, and he tells us in his preface that his notes were only taken in the last two years of Luther's life.[2] He had already begun to collect Lutherana in 1540, and by 1553 he tells us that he had 2000 of Luther's letters. As the basis of his edition of the *Tischreden* he took the fourth redaction of Lauterbach, translated the Latin words into German and added some material of his own and others. The arrangement gives no indication of the sources from which he took the various *Tischreden*, so it is impossible to say, except from internal evidence, which often cannot be applied, what notes are his own, what are

---

[1] *Cf. Realenc.*, ii, 291. Short lives of Aurifaber are given in the Introductions of Förstemann-Bindseil, Walch and Kroker.

[2] See *Supra*, p. 5.

Besold's, what Lauterbach's and others. It would be a conceivably possible, though a stupendous and almost fruitless task, to unweave the web he has woven and assign each of his sayings to its proper source, where these are already known, and distribute the residue, with some probability, to him or others according to the time in which they apparently fell.[1]

[1] The proofs of the statements, and some account of his work more in detail, will be given later.

CHAPTER IV

The Sources

In the Preface we compared the process of accumulation whereby the sayings of Luther were gathered from a large number of primary sources into a few large collections, to a great river system in which many springs send tributaries into a few great streams. This comparison, however, gives no idea of the complexity of the process, and we might make the simile more exact if we imagined a large number of canals and aqueducts taking water from each spring and conducting into a number of tributaries at once, and crossing back and forth from one stream to another until the waters of all were thoroughly mixed. The simplest way of grasping the situation is by turning to the table in the Appendix, where the relations of the MSS. and editions are plotted in such a manner as will make the method of transcription and composition of the collections clear.

It will be seen from this table that we start with the twelve men who have left us records of the Table Talk. The notes of four of these are extant in their first form, or a close copy of it. They are: Cordatus, Schlaginhaufen, Dietrich and Lauterbach. Five others, Mathesius, Plato, Besold, Heydenreich and Weller are known by transcriptions into the Mathesian collection, and sometimes elsewhere. Of the others, Corvinus has left us but one note (taken into Schlaginhaufen's book), and the sayings taken down by Stolz and Aurifaber have become inextricably blended in the collection made by the latter. Besides these notebooks, we have one source of a different kind, in the

Luther Histories of Mathesius. For convenience we shall treat the sources under the three heads: 1. The Notebooks extant in their first form. 2. The Notebooks in the Mathesian Collection. 3. The Luther Histories.

1. *The Notebooks extant in their original form*

As might be expected, the diaries in which the disciples preserved their master's sayings, show all degrees of accuracy. Their value, though in all cases superior to that of the later collections, is very unequal, depending chiefly upon three things: *a.* whether the notetaker was a rapid and good writer or not. *b.* whether he dated his notes or not. *c.* whether he put down only what he heard, or also copied from his friends. We need not consider, at this stage, the possibility of conscious falsification, either in the interests of pious edification, or for any other cause. There would be no such alteration, because, the notes being kept for private use, there would be no motive for disturbing them. Later, when they began to be published, they suffered much in this way.

The best of the notebooks is that of Lauterbach for the year 1538. In this he carefully dated every saying, and he copied little or nothing from any one else. The notebooks of Schlaginhaufen and Dietrich occupy a middle place; dates are not given for every saying, but the notes were taken chronologically and approximate dates are easily deducible for all the sayings, exact dates for many. Schlaginhaufen tells us he copied one remark from Corvinus,[1] and we suspect him of taking a few others from Dietrich and Cordatus, but only a few. Dietrich kept what he copied from others in a separate book, and hence his own notebook is free from sophistication. His notes, unfortunately not yet published, are said to show a great

---

[1] Preger, *op. cit.*, no. 342.

degree of precision.[1]   Those of Cordatus are the least reliable; he copied so much and so promiscuously that it is
hard to assign any original value to his notes except in the
cases in which they can be expressly proved to be his.   His
notebook, in fact, stands half way between a source like
that of Schlaginhaufen, and a collection, such as those we
shall consider in the next chapter.   Let us now take up the
notebooks briefly, in order.

As has been said, Cordatus was the first to think of pre-
serving the Table Talk of Luther.   His notes were not
used by Mathesius or Aurifaber in their later collections,
perhaps because Cordatus took pains to keep them from
getting into circulation, mindful of Luther's injunction to
his friends not to publish anything without his knowledge.[2]
His notebook was first found and published in 1885 by
Wrampelmeyer.[3]

Only very vague limits can be fixed as to the time
within which his notes fell.   The earliest date assignable
from internal evidence is 1524 or 1525.   The record was
closed in 1537 when Cordatus left Wittenberg, as is proved
by the naïve subscription of the man whom Cordatus employed to copy his notes, which reads: " Praise and thanks
to God that I am at the end, for I have simply written myself half to death, and yet wouldn't give up.   May God re-
store my right side which is smitten with cramp from im-
moderate writing.   1537.   Glory to God!   Finis."

---

[1] Preger, Einl., p. xxiv.

[2] As Wrampelmeyer conjectures, *op. cit.*, Einl., pp. 40, 41.

[3] From a MS. in the Library at Zellerfled.   The identity of the
author is established both by the inscription on the cover and internal
evidence, such as the use of the first person.   *E. g.*, "Ad me, cum Vit-
tenbergae agerem propter Verbum, quoties dixit: Cordate, si vos non
pecuniam habetis, &c."   See also passage quoted above (p. 14) and
Wrampelmeyer, *op. cit.*, nos. 56, 133, 133a.

The value of the source under discussion is seriously impaired by the fact that the author copied promiscuously from his contemporaries Dietrich and Schlaginhaufen, mixing, as he expresses it, their crumbs with his in a mass of pious sayings, which may be pleasing to him but is extremely puzzling to the investigator. The copying was done not at one time, and in a separate part of the book, but concurrently with the process of notetaking by the author himself. Thus we have now a note of Cordatus, then a few from Dietrich, then one or two from Schlaginhaufen and back to Cordatus again.[1]

Dietrich and Schlaginhaufen also copied something from him and from each other, but in an entirely different way, and one which does not impair the value of their notes. Cordatus copied by far the most, and mixed what he copied indistinguishably with his original material.[2]

Dietrich's extremely valuable report, which is preserved in the Nuremberg city library, still awaits an editor.[3] It has been incorrectly attributed to Mathesius on the basis of

---

[1] The question of the authenticity and chronology of Cordatus' notes is extremely intricate. Wrampelmeyer (*op. cit.*, Einl., pp. 38, 39) gives a table of dates, which shows that he thinks he can fix the time of about 100 out of nearly 2,000 sayings. I consider his table unsatisfactory. On Cordatus' relations to Dietrich, Schlaginhaufen and Lauterbach (from whom he copied very much), see Kroker, Einl., p. 55; Preger, *op. cit.*, pp. xxiv-xxvi. Cordatus was immensely overestimated by Wrampelmeyer; he is, perhaps, unduly depreciated by the later investigators.

[2] Schlaginhaufen copied little; Dietrich kept what he copied separate from what he took himself.

[3] Seidemann prepared this MS. for the press, but died before printing was actually begun. Köstlin used it in Seidemann's copy. *Cf.* Wrampelmeyer, *op. cit.*, p. 27, note 1. Köstlin, *op. cit.*, Vorwort to second edition, and vol. i, p. 774, vol. ii, p. 487. Dietrich's *notes* are discussed here, his *collection*, an entirely different book, in the next chapter.

an inscription on the binding, but internal evidence proves that Dietrich was the author.[1] On close examination Preger found he could date the individual notes, at least approximately. In their present form they are part of a manuscript which contains other material also. It has been proved that the part containing the Table Talk is simply bound in with the other material, and not copied with it from a common source by the same scribe. In binding, the quires of the notebook were disarranged; they originally followed one another in chronological order, which was restored by Preger.[2]

The conversations reported fall, as is stated in the title, within the years 1529-1535; the great majority of them demonstrably within the years 1531-1533.[3]

---

[1] The inscription is, " Mathesii αὐτόγραφον." This is certainly an error, probably caused by some half-obliterated words on the parchment binding, of which " Mathesii " is one of the few still legible. These words very likely contained some expression of Mathesius, or some quotation from him; whatever they may mean, it is certain the MS. is from Dietrich's notes. For proof, cf. Preger, op. cit., Einl., p. xviii. Also Seidemann, Sächsische Kirch- und Schulblatt, 1876, no. 43. Lösche, Analecta, p. 10. Köstlin, op. cit., vol. 1, p. 224, note 3.

[2] They are contained in pp. 33-200 of this MS. The notation of the quires is E-DD. An older notation, represented by the small letters, b-q, can be discerned, which lettering is found only on the sheets which have Tischreden. The order, mixed in the binding, was restored by Preger, quem vide, op. cit., Einl., pp. xix-xxi. There is an Appendix of quires, F, G and H, which have no small letters. They probably contain copies from Dietrich's collection, and not, properly, his own notes. They puzzled Preger, who did not know that Dietrich kept a separate book for copies. Cf. infra, next chapter.

[3] The dates are ascertainable partly by marginal notes, partly by internal evidence, such as reference to some contemporary event. Preger gives the dates and evidence, op. cit., Einl., pp. xix-xx. He thinks the reference to the happy estate of the peasants points to the good harvest of 1530. It seems to me that the reference is rather to the good fortune of peasants in general in being free from temptation. The other indications used by Preger in dating appear to me perfectly sound.

Schlaginhaufen's book of Table Talk was discovered in a MS. in the Munich Library and edited by Preger in 1888.[1] It appears to be almost entirely original, though the author tells us he got one saying from Corvinus (no. 342), and another (no. 142) appears to have been copied also, perhaps from Dietrich or Cordatus. As we have just seen, Schlaginhaufen was much copied by them.

His notes fall in the years 1531-1532, and were taken by him in chronological order.[2] Schlaginhaufen is one of the most accurate and conscientious of the reporters, giving not only the substance but the exact form of Luther's words, as nearly as possible. Careful as he was, however, we can see that at times he wrote from memory, and not, as usually, on the spot, " just as if at a lecture." For example, the long exhortation by which Luther assisted him to recover from his swoon (no. 57) could not have been taken at the time, when he would have been in no condition to write. We have a curious indication, however, that it was written down the next day.[3] In other cases it is natural to suppose that details of time, place and circumstance were added later.

Lauterbach was the author of a large number of books of Luther's Table Talk. These books may be divided into two classes, the notebooks (*Tagebücher*), in which he first entered the sayings as he heard them at table, and the collections, in which he afterwards edited and arranged

---

[1] *Ibid.*, Einl., p. v, proves the MS. to be from Schlaginhaufen's notes.

[2] *Ibid.*, Einl., pp. xv, xvi.

[3] This is that when Cordatus copied it he dated it the day after it happened, probably copying the day of its entry rather than the day of its occurrence. In general, the accuracy of Schlaginhaufen is seen by the roughness of his notes. Kroker, *op. cit.*, (Einl., p. 3,) suggests this may have been due to the fact that Schlaginhaufen could not write as fast as Dietrich.

his raw material. He never did this in a way which permanently satisfied him, and so we have four redactions of the great edition. They will be discussed later, in the chapter on the collections. His early books of *Tischreden* may again be divided into two classes, those which he kept for his own notations, and those in which he copied what was taken down by his friends (we have called one of these his simple collection as opposed to his large edition, spoken of above.) Of the former class we possess one, the *Tagebuch of 1538*, in a close copy of the original, and two others, one containing material compiled during the years 1536 and 1537, and one for 1539, in the form in which they were later incorporated into the Mathesian Collection.[1]

The *Tagebuch of 1538* is by far the most accurate source we have. It begins on January 1 and goes to December 12, dating each entry exactly, though not containing an entry for every day. Luther's words are put down in their exact form, the mixture of Latin and German which he used being retained. For his own remarks Lauterbach generally employs Latin, as the easier of the languages to write quickly.[2]

The notes are full as well as accurate. Lauterbach spent no less conscientious toil on them than Rörer did on his reports of Luther's sermons. From them and from Luther's letters we can get a clear and detailed picture of just what the reformer was doing and thinking every day of the year 1538.

---

[1] The relations of the sources to the later collections is made clear in the Appendix.

[2] This Tagebuch was edited by Seidemann in 1872. In his Preface (pp. iii and xiii) the editor proves the accuracy of the notes. A later critic discovers some omissions, *cf.* W. Meyer: "Ueber Lauterbachs und Aurifabers Sammlungen der Tischreden Luthers" in *Abhandlungen der königlichen Gesellschaften der Wissenschaften zu Göttingen, Phil. Hist. Klasse*, Neue Folge, 1897, vol. i, no. 2, p. 37.

The rapidity of writing caused some errors, and is constantly betrayed in the rough style of the notes.[1] Thousands of changes are made in the later collections in the material taken from this with the desire to improve the literary form and sometimes the sense also. For example, it is recounted of a locksmith's apprentice, how he saw an evil spirit which chased him for several hours one evening through the streets of Wittenberg and asked him whether he believed the catechism and why he had taken the Lord's Supper in both kinds, and forbade him to return to his master's house, which he therefore shunned for some days. Lauterbach and others brought him to Luther, who said, " We must not believe every one, because many are imposters." In the later collection the sense is completely altered; it is not the devil, but Luther who questions the young man on his faith.[2]

Lauterbach's notes for 1536-7 were absorbed into Weller's collection and with it taken into the Mathesian collection.[3] His notes of 1539 have survived in a copy made by the Rev. Paul Richter in 1553-1554. From this a small selection was made and incorporated into the Mathesian collection.[4]

[1] *E. g.*, Seidemann, *op. cit.*, p. 44. "3 Martii Luther habebat convivium sui regni. Ibi coenabantur, recitabantur psalmi evangelia catechismus orationes prout singulis erat demandatum; sed familia in pronunciando respirebat." Here *respirebat* is senseless and *coenabantur* is strange. In the MSS. *Wer.* and *Mun.* (see Appendix), and in Bindseil these words are corrected to *haesitabat* and *canabantur* respectively. Meyer, *loc. cit.*, p. 38. Meyer is criticising Seidemann's editing.

[2] As given in the *Tagebuch* it is undoubtedly correct, though Luther's response is inconsistent with his usually credulous attitude. Other examples given in Meyer, *loc. cit.*, p. 37. The anecdote is given in Seidemann, *op. cit.*, p. 6, for Jan. 10.

[3] Secs. 4 and 5 of Kroker's *Tischreden in der Mathesischen Sammlung.* See *infra*.

[4] Sec. 6 of Kroker. For Richter, see Appendix on MSS. His MS. is called *Colloquia Serotina*.

2. Notebooks which have survived in the Mathesian Collection

Besides the notebooks of the four men discussed in the first part of this chapter we have notes of Mathesius, Heydenreich, Besold and Weller, which were taken in part into the Mathesian collection. Mathesius made his collection on a different plan from those of Lauterbach and Aurifaber, who took the notes out of their original order and rearranged them topically. Mathesius copied his sources one after the other, so that we can distinguish the contributions of each, date the notes and estimate their relative value. But though the Mathesian collection is divided into sections corresponding with the sources from which the editor copied, he does not tell us who is the author of each particular one, and the nice work of discrimination has to be based upon internal evidence. Kroker, who has edited Mathesius, has done the work admirably, and our account will follow him. Leaving the features which are common to the whole collection to be dealt with later, we shall now proceed to speak briefly of the individual notebooks which compose it.

The most important of these is Mathesius' own *Tagebuch*, printed by the editor as the first section of the collection.[1] The sayings fall in the months of May to November (except July, when Luther was away) of the year 1540. The order is that in which Mathesius took them down from day to day. The reporter did not take the trouble to date every entry he made, as did Lauterbach, but from the dates given and those deducible we can assign each saying to very nearly the proper day. Entries are not made every day, but there are some omissions, the longest of which are for the month of July, when Luther went to

---

[1] Evidence for the dates of the sayings given, Kroker, *op. cit.*, Einl., p. 27.

Weimar and Eisenach, and at the end of August, when either Mathesius may have left for a short time—Luther's beer had given out—,[1] or else he remitted his activity in taking notes because of Käthe's sharp reflection on the practice, recorded by Mathesius [2] in the following anecdote:

When somebody asked the Doctor a question his wife said jestingly, " Doctor, don't teach them free! For they have already learned much so, Lauterbach the most and the best." The Doctor answered, " I have taught and preached freely for thirty years; why should I begin to charge now?"

The other notes which have come down to us in this collection are of less importance. Those of Plato will be treated more fully in the next chapter, as they resemble a collection more than they do a notebook. A large and valuable selection from Heydenreich's notes of the years 1542 and 1543 is given in the second section of the Mathesian collection as printed by Kroker. Only excerpts were taken by Mathesius, as is proved by the fact that all the jokes, which must have been present, as they are so frequent in Mathesius' own notes, are omitted as unimportant.[3]

Besold's notes (a few poor ones only have survived) from the year 1544 are taken into the third section of Kroker's [4] edition of Mathesius. Weller's notes also form a section of this work. He kept two books, one of which we may call a notebook, and one a collection, though there

---

[1] Kroker, *op. cit.*, no. 417, August 24.

[2] *Ibid.*, no. 332. See also no. 334, note.

[3] There are 158 sayings of Heydenreich dated by the superscription 1542. Kroker (*op. cit.*, Einl., p. 40) proves some of them to have been from 1543. He proves in the same place that the section comes from Heydenreich. The sequence of the sayings was disturbed, just as in the cases of Dietrich and Schlaginhaufen, in the binding.

[4] Sec. 3 of Kroker's *Mathesius*, no. 260-271, Einl., p. 44.

is not much difference between them. He copied much from Lauterbach in both, and we have to distinguish the source of each by internal evidence.[1]

3. The Luther Histories of Mathesius

Besides the sayings which have come down to us in the notebooks we have just been discussing, quite a number have survived in a different sort of a work where they are introduced casually, and do not constitute the main interest. This work is a series of " Sermons," or lectures, on Luther's life, published by Mathesius thirty years after he had ceased to take notes at Luther's table. Even after this stretch of time, the author was able to remember and recount some sayings of Luther which are found nowhere else, and for which, therefore, these lectures must be considered the source. It is easy to see how much less weight can be given to this than to the other sources which were written on the spot. Let us see how far Mathesius was dependent on his memory, and how far on his own, or others', previous notes.[2]

If we compare Mathesius' collection with his sermons we see that a great deal of material is common to both. Hardly a page of the latter is without some parallel in the former, parallels to his own notes of 1540 being especially

[1] Weller's notebook, sec. 4, Kroker; his collection, sec. 8. See Kroker, op. cit., p. 45.

[2] The relation of the Luther Histories and Mathesius' notes was touched upon by Lösche (Analecta, Einl., p. 32), but he thought it not worth considering, as he found only eight parallels. Had he taken short sentences and clauses, which are evidently reminiscences of the notes, as well as the elaborate parallels, he might have made a much larger list. Kroker did this, and found over one hundred parallels to the collection, of which 80 were to Mathesius' own notes; besides this he found parallels to others—Dietrich, Lauterbach and Schlaginhaufen. For the Luther Histories, see Appendix.

frequent.[1] Are these parallels due to the fact that he re-
members the sayings he inserts independently, or to the fact
that he read them from his collection? We notice that he
seldom quotes with verbal exactness, which proves, at least,
that he did not have the collection before him as he talked.
A further analysis shows three kinds of agreement, varying
by degree of closeness. (*a*) Agreement of form and expression, which is very rare. When we find it, it is in short,
characteristic expressions. Mathesius has the same pen-
chant for enlarging on what Luther said, that we discover
in Lauterbach and Aurifaber. (*b*) Agreement in content,
with difference in expression. This is the rule. Luther's
sayings are ornamented and the circumstances of their ut-
terance given. Sometimes there is nothing to distinguish
Luther's words from Mathesius' own remarks.[2] (*c*)
Sometimes the sense as well as the form is changed.[3]

It is but natural that much of the material in the ser-

[1] Kroker, *op. cit.*, Einl., p. 67. As sources, Mathesius also used the
Wittenberg edition of Luther's writings and Aurifaber's of his letters.
Aurifaber's *Tischreden* had not yet appeared.

[2] Kroker gives examples, *op. cit.*, Einl., p. 69. The most important
one is the story of the Elbe turning red, which is recounted in three
separate documents by Mathesius, *viz.:* 1. A letter to Spalatin. 2.
Tischreden, Kroker, *op. cit.*, no. 120. 3. In the *Luther Histories*. On
their face these three accounts contradict each other; in one source
Luther knows nothing certain of the facts, in another he has seen it;
in one he thinks it a natural phenomenon, in another miraculous.
Kroker tries to reconcile them all, but not successfully. The case really
shows how unreliable is an account given from memory many years
after.

[3] Kroker gives examples, *op. cit.*, Einl., p. 71. One of these is Kroker,
ibid., no. 135. "Ego tres malos canes habeo, ingratitudinem, superbiam,
invidiam," etc., where it seems that Luther is referring to his own
temptations. In *Luther Histories*, lxii, 136b, the same words are used,
but applied to the clergy under him. Kroker thinks the later account
the true one, as the more probable; it seems to me that we ought to
follow the earlier even at the cost of making Luther accuse himself of
being tempted.

mons and in the notebook should be the same. Mathesius would remember what he had heard and written down previously. But by the variation in the two reports we see that one was not taken from the other. Besides there is much material in the sermons which comes from the years in which Mathesius no longer took notes. For such material the sermons are a source. Not being taken down at the time, however, and varying considerably from the material which was taken down at the time, they have less authenticity and authority than the notebooks.

CHAPTER V

The Collections

Besides taking notes of their own, many of the reporters were diligent collectors of notes taken by others. Sometimes they kept these separate from their own, sometimes they put what they copied along with their own original material. Sometimes the collections were kept in the form in which they were found in the original, sometimes they were " edited," *i. e.* smoothed off and rearranged in some definite order, usually topical. On the basis of the way in which they were collected we can, for the sake of convenience, divide the collections into three classes.

a. Mixed, *i. e.* those in which the reporter put down notes from other sources along with his own original ones promiscuously and with no attempt at order. It is hard to distinguish these collections from the notebooks, and the distinction must be somewhat arbitrary, based on the relative importance and quantity of the original and the copied notes. Cordatus, for example, had such a book, but as his own notes are in fairly large quantity and greater in importance than the copied ones, we found it convenient to consider his book as a notebook. Plato and Weller left books much like his, but in them the amount of original material is relatively so much smaller that we may consider them rather as collections than as notebooks.

b. Simple, *i. e.* those in which the author kept the notes he copied distinct from his own. Such were made by Dietrich, Lauterbach and Mathesius.

c. Edited, *i. e.* those in which the material was much changed, the notes rearranged and polished. Such was the collection known as *Farrago literarum* and such were the great collections of Lauterbach (not to be confounded with his simple one) and of Aurifaber.

We shall speak of each of the collections in turn.

That of Plato is uninteresting and of little value except as illustrating the vicissitudes through which the sayings of Luther might go before they reach us. He made the compilation chiefly by copying freely from Mathesius' note-book of 1540.[1] When Mathesius was making a collection of his own, he got hold of Plato's, most of which was taken from his own notes, and reincorporated it into his own collection, thereby duplicating some 135 sayings which he already had in their original form. Plato also copied from Dietrich, Lauterbach, and perhaps Stolz and Aurifaber, and made some slight attempt to put the sayings in topical order. The work has survived in two other copies. Melanchthon chanced to get a copy, and when he was lecturing to a class on Luther some years after his death, he took large portions of Plato as a text. These lectures were taken down by a student named Vendenhaimer, and have found their way into the *Corpus Reformatorum* along with Melanchthon's works.[2]

Weller's record of the table talk is also more famous for

---

[1] The three copies in which Plato's collection has survived are those known as *Memorabilia, Melanchthon,* and *Mathesius,* sec. 7. Kroker proved Plato to be the author, *op. cit.,* Einl., pp. 48-54. How much he copied from Mathesius is seen by the fact that of 149 sayings in the *Mathesian Collection,* 135 had been taken from Mathesius' notes of 1540.

[2] See Appendix, p. 115, for *Corpus Reformatorum.*

its complicated history and obscure method of compilation than for any value it has as an original text. We have already discussed his note book, which approaches a collection in form, as it consists largely of copies from Lauterbach. In like manner his collection has a number of original notes. Both have survived only in the copy by Mathesius, the former in Section 4 and the latter in Section 8 (as printed by Kroker).

Weller's larger work was not incorporated in the Mathesian collection by Mathesius himself, but by the man who copied it, Krüginger. As printed by Kroker, Weller's copied notes form the eighth section of the compilation called by the name of Mathesius; in the MS. which he edited it is the first. This is because Weller had been first copied by Krüginger, who made his work the first part of a new collection of his own and copied that of Mathesius as the second part. As Krüginger was a mere copyist, we always speak of the total result as the Mathesian collection, although it must be remembered that properly only sections 1-7 as printed or 2-8 as in the MS., were compiled by Mathesius himself.[1]

To return to Weller. We can discover three sections in his aggregation of notes, the first of which consists chiefly of copies from Lauterbach (and perhaps Cordatus),[2] the second, mostly of selections from Lauterbach's *Tagebuch* of 1536-7,[3] and the third, of excerpts from Dietrich and Lau-

[1] The complicated proof that Weller was the original of this collection, and that Krüginger copied it as a whole and did not compile it himself from the originals, is given by Kroker, *op. cit.*, Einl., pp. 54, 55.

[2] Parallels are found both in Cordatus and Lauterbach's great collection. The parallels in Cordatus are best explained by saying that Cordatus copied from Lauterbach's notes, which he later took into his great Collection. Kroker, *op. cit.*, Einl., p. 57.

[3] *Ibid.*, Einl., p. 58. There are no notes for February, 1537, when Luther was at Schmalkalden.

terbach, with a few original notes of Weller's own.[1]
The date of compilation was probably 1537 or 1538.

The simplest of the " simple " collection is that of
Dietrich, of which nothing need to said but that it contains
copies from Cordatus, Schlaginhaufen and Lauterbach
made in the same years in which Dietrich was taking notes
himself, *viz.* 1529-1535, and that it has survived only in
imperfect copies of portions made by three persons, one of
whom was Mathesius, who made it part of the 6th section
of his work.[2]

Lauterbach's simple collection (we must again warn the
reader not to confuse it with his notebooks on the one hand
or his great edition on the other) is extant in three MSS. as
an appendix to his *Tagebuch* of 1538. It has never been
edited, and indeed is not worth editing. All or most of it
was taken into his great edition later, when the contents
were polished and rearranged. It seems to be quite complete, containing copies from almost all the earlier group
of reporters and perhaps some of the later. It was probably made in 1538 or 1539 soon after Lauterbach left Wittenberg.[3]

---

[1] *Ibid.*, pp. 60-65. A few parallels to the third division are found
in Weller's works. They are of the kind known as *Trostschriften;*
one on a woman in spasms, one on the devil and the jurists—person-
ages who had a peculiarly close relationship in Luther's mind.

[2] *Ibid.*, Einl., p. 46. The other MSS. which contain excerpts from it
are those we have called *Bavarus* and *Obenander.* See Appendix. Some
copies are made from an otherwise unknown and unidentifiable source.

[3] The MSS. which contain this collection are *Khumer*, pp. 257-426,
Wer., pp. 35-212b, and *Mun clm 939*, pp. 7b-116b. The whole subject is
discussed by Meyer, *loc. cit.*, p. 40. Seidemann, who edited the *Tagebuch* of 1538 read these notes, which he says also come from Lauterbach's notes (Seidemann, *op. cit.*, Einl., pp. ix, x). He seems to have
thought, however, that they were in some way collected by the author

The compilation of Mathesius, in the form of an appendix to his own notes of 1540, is the largest we have, being, in fact, a collection of collections. As it now stands (in the printed edition of Kroker from Krüginger's copy) it consists of eight sections, each section corresponding to the notes copied from one of the author's sources. Each source was taken and copied straight through, with no attempt to rearrange the notes. These sections are:

1. Mathesius' own notes of 1540.
2. Heydenreich's notes of 1542-1543.
3. Besold's notes of 1544.
4. Weller's notebook (with copies from Lauterbach, see *supra*).
5. Lauterbach's notebook of 1539.
6. Copies from the notebook and collection of Dietrich.
7. Plato's collection.
8. Weller's collection.

The accumulation of these sources was gradual. Mathesius started with his own notes of 1540 and after Luther's death added to them notes from others one by one as he came across them, those of Heydenreich and Besold in 1547, the next two sections in 1548 and the seventh some time later. The eighth section was not in Mathesius' own collection but was added by the copyist, Krüginger.[1]

---

of the MS., *Khumer, viz.*, Khumer, a friend of Lauterbach's. This could not have been so, however, as Khumer's MS. dates from 1554, and the collection had already been copied 1550 in *Mun. clm. 939*. In general, the notes agree in form closely with the later great collection of which they formed a chief source.

[1] This section was one which had been copied by Krüginger from Weller before he got Mathesius' collection, and was made by him the first section of the collection as it now stands in the Leipzig MS. Kroker, who edited the MS. in 1903, restored the order of Mathesius and printed (or rather summarized) Krüginger's own collection in the 8th section. *Cf. supra*, p. 37, on Weller's collection.

A greater contrast in the treatment of the same material
than that between the original notes and early copies of the
Table Talk, and the later polished, or " edited " collections can hardly be imagined. The notes were taken
roughly and hastily at first, in transcription they were
somewhat altered, abbreviations were expanded, omissions
filled in, smooth forms substituted for rough, one language
for the mixture of two and grammatical for ungrammatical
constructions. These changes were begun by the reporters
in copying their own notes, but they were extremely slight
compared to the changes made by the later editors.

In the original notes the chronological order is the one
usually followed, and there is no attempt to replace it by
the topical. In the edited collections the material is cut
up and redistributed, explanations are added, much is
omitted and much entirely recast. The idea was no longer
to give a faithful report of Luther's exact words, it was to
make an edifying book, something which would serve
partly as a repertory for anecdotes to be used in sermons,
partly as a pious memorial of Luther. All obscurities were
cleared up, whatever was coarse was softened down, and
whatever would give ground to the enemies of the faith
was attenuated. Sometimes changes were made in the interest of picquancy, sometimes the original was misunderstood.[1] Dates and circumstances were added from memory,
often incorrectly.

[1] An interesting example of this is found in the story related in its
original form by Cordatus (Wrampelmeyer, *op. cit.*, 945) and taken
(either from him or some other source) into a later collection (Förstemann-Bindseil, *Tischreden*, i, p. 293). In Cordatus it is: " Et Maxi-
milianus valde suspiciosus fuit in re militari. Gentes in periculis mac-
taverunt etiam dilectissima," etc. Luther was thinking of such cases
as Iphigenia, but the application of his words directly to Maximilian
lead to the following amusing translation: " Kaiser Maximilian soll in
Kriegshändeln sehr abergläubish gewesen sein; in Fährlichkeiten thät
er Gott Gelübde und schlachtete was ihm am ersten begegnet, wie man
von ihm saget."

One MS. preserves an early attempt to compile such a book by an unknown author, which, though neither large nor good, nor historically important, is interesting as showing the first case of the topical redaction which added so greatly to the value of the book for purposes of edification. The MS. was written in 1551 by " M. B." and is called *Farrago literarum ad amicos et colloquiorum in mensa R. P. Domini Martini Lutheri.*[1]

It was the most assiduous of the reporters who became the most diligent of the redactors and collectors. Lauterbach had a vast quantity of original notes as well as a collection containing copies from other reporters. These he kept by him until 1558 (twenty years after the bulk of them had been taken) and then he decided to put them all into a single volume, neatly polished and topically arranged. This great work took him two years, and when it was done he was not satisfied with it but worked it over three times within the course of the next two years *i. e.* 1560-1562. We shall say just a word about each of the redactions to show his method of procedure and its effect upon the Table Talk.[2]

The first edition of the great collection was made, as has been said, in the years 1558-1560.[3] The arrangement is somewhat peculiar. After cutting up Luther's sayings in tiny sections with separate titles, he combined them into large groups under general captions. He began by arranging these groups according to his idea of the relative

[1] See Köstlin, *op. cit.*, vol. i, p. 774; Kroker, *op. cit.*, p. 6, note 1.

[2] My account is taken entirely from W. Meyer: " Ueber Lauterbachs und Aurifabers Sammlungen der Luthers Tischreden," in *Abhandlungen d. k. Gesellschaft der Wissenschaften z. Göttingen, Phil. Hist. Kl., Neue Folge*, Bd. i, no. 2, 1897. For these redactions, see pp. 9-18.

[3] MS. in Halle edited by Bindseil in three vols., 1860-63, see Appendix.

importance of their subjects from a theological standpoint.
Thus the first chapter treated God, the second the Bible
and so on. After a while all the important points of doctrine had been disposed of and he came to a lot of chapters
treating of matters indifferent. These he arranged in alphabetic order, making them the second and third volume
of his collection.[1]

Lauterbach's second edition of his collection was made
shortly after the first was completed.[2] Its peculiarity consists in the rearrangement of the small sections in the larger
chapters.[3] Many passages are omitted, some material is
added though not much. The chief addition is that of
introductions to many sections by Lauterbach himself, giving circumstances and explanations. These he may have
taken from notes, but more probably added from memory.

The third redaction we do not know in a good copy, but
only in Rebenstock's edition in which all the German is
turned into Latin. This was completed about 1561.[4] Its
characteristic is that the chapters or chief divisions are
rearranged. These changes were in part intentional, in
part due to carelessness, a section omitted by oversight in
one place being inserted at another. A good example of

---

[1] This order was misunderstood and confused by the copyist. It has
been restored by Meyer.

[2] Preserved in two copies in MSS. at *Dresden* and *Gotha*, see Appendix.

[3] E. g., under chapter " Civitas " all the sayings about each particular
state are brought together.

[4] Rebenstock says he took it (1571) from a MS. "*ante annos 10 ad
aeditionem parata.*" Bindseil, vol. i, Einl., pp. lxxxi-c. He was much
puzzled by the relation of Rebenstock to this MS. The date of the
second redaction should have been 1561. The Gotha MS. has 1562, but
that may only refer to the time when it was copied from Lauterbach's
original. Or both the third and second redactions may have been 1562;
Rebenstock's 10 years being simply approximate.

the first kind of change is the grouping the chapters *Anti-nomi, Anabaptistae, Antichrist, Papae, Papistate* and *Papatus* all together under the head of Luther's enemies, the intention being, of course, to get a more logical order. An example of the other kind of change is found in the insertion of the chapter *"Absolutio,"*—which had been accidentally omitted before,—between the sections on "Luther" and " Melanchthon." Such an oversight is made possible by the fact that Lauterbach distributed his notes into quires, and his arrangement consisted in making a new arrangement of these; when a quire was mislaid it was left out of its proper place, and inserted later, when found.

Another striking characteristic of the third redaction (and also of the fourth, which may have been copied from it) is the recurrence of numerous and important omissions. In some cases these were undoubtedly intentional, as they are of irrelevant passages,[1] in other cases no such reason can be assigned, and the omissions must have been due to carelessness or accident. The arrangement of the last half of Part I and the whole of Part II is the old alphabetic one.

The fourth redaction is known to us in the Wolfen-büttel MS. of 1562. As it was the one taken by Aurifaber as the basis of his printed edition, we will discuss it later when we come to him and his relation to Lauterbach.[2]

The differences between these four editions are far too great to be accounted for by any vagary of a copyist or scribe. They imply conscious redaction. We are sure that Lauterbach was the redactor of the first three editions, and probably of the fourth, though the proof for it is not clear as that may have been an early attempt of Aurifaber.[3]

---

[1] Meyer, pp. 12, 13. On pp. 14-17 he gives a long list of text changes in the various redactions. [2] *Infra*, p. 62.

[3] Bindseil (Colloq., vol. i, Einl., p. xxxxix) proved that Lauterbach

Lauterbach's method of working is interesting. We see by comparison of the original sources with his version of them in his great collection that he changed not a little. In his first notes we see how scrupulously careful he was to get the exact form of Luther's words. He changed this a good deal in his first edition of the collection, and even after that, with the intention of improvement. He doubtless felt that the way in which the sayings had been reported was not absolutely definitive. His changes were not confined to supposed textual emendations, but were often made with the manifest purpose of edification, and especially of eliminating whatever might damage the character of his hero.[1]

He took no care, however, to avoid repetitions, and many an old " grouse in the gun-room " story of Luther's meets us in several places. Sometimes he combined entirely different stories to get a good narration. Sometimes he deliberately falsified the text in the interests of piety. Even though his motive was good his lack of literary tact and discrimination made the text worse when he changed it. He was encouraged to change because, having taken notes himself, he was aware that it was hard to get the exact form of Luther's expressions, and therefore corrected them in accord with principles which he supposed would bring out the true sense.

The most famous of all the collections, and, until within

was the collector of the first redaction. Meyer (pp. 19, 20) goes over his reasons and proves the 2d and 3d redactions to be by Lauterbach. This certainty is worth something, as it gives a little more authority to changes than if they had been by some one else.

[1] Meyer, pp. 20-25. Besides *Tischreden*, Lauterbach mixed in some extraneous material, such as *e. g.*, letters and allegories related by Melanchthon. Meyer found parallels to some of them in old MS. collections of allegories.

fifty years the only one (except Rebenstock's edition, which has always been scarce) to be printed, is that made by Aurifaber. He had begun collecting materials for it with a view to editing at least ten years,[1] indeed one may say twenty years before it came out, when he sat at Luther' table and took notes of his sayings along with the other students. It may have been that he met Lauterbach at this time, when the latter came for a short visit from Pirna where he was pastor.

It was not until about 1561, however, that he really began to think of using the material he had accumulated for an edition of *Tischreden*. In that year his quarrel with Chancellor Brück compelled him to take refuge with his former patron the Count of Mansfeld, and the five years of enforced leisure which followed he used to good advantage in literary labors. He was doubtless encouraged to publish the *Tischreden* by the success his edition of the letters had attained. The materials in his hands were not copious, and to supplement them he turned to Lauterbach whose reputation as the best of the notetakers was already well established. In 1562 he got hold of one of Lauterbach's redactions—though just how is not known. He knew it was Lauterbach's, for he mentions him in his preface as his chief source, and it is probable that Lauterbach himself gave it to him, for he had just completed it himself, and there would hardly have been time for an intermediary copy.[2]

---

[1] In the Introduction to his edition of Luther's letters, vol. i, which came out 1556, he tells us that he had already been collecting: *"Lutheri enarrationes in aliquot libros biblicos, multorum annorum conciones, disputationes, concilia, colloquia & epistolas."*

[2] The general similarity and numerous minor differences between Rebenstock, the Halle MS. and Aurifaber puzzled investigators like Bindseil, who did not know the history of the redactions, first worked out by Meyer.

In the MS. at Wolfenbüttel mentioned above we have a fragment of what is either a fourth redaction by Lauterbach, or, what is more probable, an early attempt by Aurifaber. It is extremely interesting as being something between Lauterbach's earlier redactions, and the collection of Aurifaber, as we know it in print. It contains only 168 sayings, all translated into German in Aurifaber's manner. He appears to have omitted the introductions and extra material put into his third redaction by Lauterbach, which would go to show that he copied one of the first two. All the material in this MS. was incorporated later into his printed edition by Aurifaber.

Aurifaber was so much pleased with Lauterbach's redaction that he adopted it as the basis of his whole work, and did not change its form much. He translated all the material into the vernacular, and occasionally would improve Lauterbach's account by means of another.[1] Sometimes the same saying crept in twice. Almost all the material can be traced to its source, by far the greater part in Lauterbach, a little to other sources. The irreducible minimum, for which no previous authority can be found, comes from Aurifaber's own notes, or from what he had copied of Stolz.[2]

---

[1] Example, Aurifaber, ch. 13, no. 39, where Lauterbach's account (Bindseil, i, 59) is corrected by Schlaginhaufen's (Preger, no. 522).

[2] Bindseil noted at the end of his third volume the passages translated from Lauterbach in the German *Tischreden;* every new research shows more parallels between this edition and the sources. *Cf.* Meyer, p. 33.

CHAPTER VI

The Printed Editions of the Table Talk

The result of all this collecting and editing was seen at last in July, 1566, when the stout folio appeared at Eisleben. Aurifaber placed the arms of the Counts of Mansfeld on the reverse of the title-page, and dedicated the result of his labors comprehensively to " Den Edelen, Ehrenuesten, Erbarn und Wolweisen, Ammeistern, Stadtpflegern, Eldtern, Geheimbten, Bürgermeistern, und Rath, Der Keisserlichen Reichstedte, Strassburg, Augsburg, Ulm, Norimberg, Lubeck, Hamburg, Lüneburg, Braunschweig, Franckforth am Mayn, und Regensburg, &c., Meinen grossgünstigen Herrn."

The Preface tells how the *Tischreden* were collected, and gives an exalted appreciation of their value in satisfying " geistlichen Hunger und Durst." [1] They at once became immensely popular, and were reprinted from this edition in five years at least six times. Two of the new editions were pirated, and in his own reprint of 1568 Aurifaber bitterly complains of this. The book has been exploited, he says, by " Master Klügling, who entered into my labors, changed the title and altered much in the book, at sundry times enlarging and (supposedly) improving it with new sayings, all without my knowledge or approval. . . . But let every one know that if there is any one who can improve or add

---

[1] Förstemann-Bindseil, *op. cit.*, vol. iv, p. xxiii *et seq.* See Appendix for list of editions.

to the *Tischreden,* it is I, (I can say it without vainglory) for I have enough in MS. to make a new volume, or at least greatly enlarge my first one." [1]

The changes referred to by Aurifaber are hardly so great as to justify his language about them. That of the title is simply the insertion of Lauterbach's name along with that of Aurifaber, certainly justifiable from the amount he contributed to it.[2] The other additions and " improvements " are very slight; it is to Aurifaber's interest, of course to exaggerate the faults of " Master Klügling " in order to enhance the genuine worth of his own reprints.

The next editor was Rebenstock, who got hold of one of Lauterbach's redactions and translated the whole thing into Latin. His edition never enjoyed much popularity, and is now excessively rare. It was used somewhat outside of Germany; for example, if we may believe a French translator of the Table Talk, by the great Bayle.[3] The work came out in 1571 in two octavo volumes.

There is a preface of Rebenstock in a letter to Philip Ludwig, Count of Hanoia and Rineck, Lord of Mintzenberg. It is a long exhortation, mingled with sacred history and ending with a eulogy of Luther. As to the Colloquies he is editing he says:

A certain pious man, a lover of the Evangelic truth, wrote Martin Luther's *Colloquies* in Latin, but mixed in many German words. . . . . And when the printers, by the advice of

----

[1] *Ibid.,* pp. xxvi, xxvii.

[2] The changes are, in fact, so small that Bindseil (*ibid.*) did not think Aurifaber could be referring to them, and looked in vain for some other edition which would correspond to his language more accurately. It seems to me, however, that it must have been the editions of 1567 which he referred to, though he made them out worse than they really were.

[3] Brunet, Introduction to his *Propos de Table.*

learned men, wished to publish the colloquies in Latin, they asked me to turn the German words into Latin. . . . I never proposed to undertake this labor, however, in order to defile Luther's pious sayings with other impious and unedifying ones, or to add new ones, or to acquire glory and profit to myself (as the Sacramentarians and Ranters of to-day presume to do), but I proposed to render our master his praise, and so, aided by the counsel of learned men, I entered upon the work. . . .

Dated " Ex Cinericea doma, in die S. Laurentii, 1571," and signed " H. P. Rebenstock Escherheymensis Ecclesiae minister." [1]

This Preface would seem to show that Rebenstock was a mere linguistic aid, and not an editor in the proper sense of the word.[2] He either did not know, or did not reveal, the name of the " pius vir " who made the collection, but he says in his preface that it was not Aurifaber. We, of course, know that it was Lauterbach.

The first editor to compete with Aurifaber in a German edition was Stangwald, Candidate of Theology in Prussia. He printed a first edition in 1571 and a second in 1591. He took Aurifaber's material, but arranged it in a different way, instead of the eighty chapters of Aurifaber, we have nine great unnumbered divisions, and forty-three chapters under these. He claims to have used Mörlin's notations to the MS. of Aurifaber, as well as the notes of Mathesius and others, and also to have excised some sayings which he believed unauthentic. His changes, were, however, very slight indeed.[3]

---

[1] Bindseil, vol. i, p. lxx. [2] *Cf.* Meyer, *loc. cit.*, p. 6.

[3] Irmischer, *Tischreden* in *Sämmtliche Werke Luthers*, vol. 57, Einl., pp. xii-xiv. A full description of all the editions will be found in the Appendix. This present chapter aims to give a brief account of each edition, and some suggestions as to the critical principles to be applied in getting a good edition.

Nicholaus Selneccer (or Selnecker) was the next editor.
His edition come out in 1577. He recognized in his title
that the *Tischreden* were first collected by Aurifaber, and
he claims to have brought them into a new order and added
an index. These claims are unjustified. He merely reprints Stangwald's edition of 1571, which had changed the
order in Aurifaber's. He was enabled to make this claim by
the fact that Stangwald had not put his name on the title
page of his edition of 1571, and it is only by his allusion
to it in his subsequent edition that we know it was his. It
was once a question whether this was really his edition or
Selneccer's; it is now settled that it is Stangwald's.[1]

The first editor to make the German *Tischreden* a part
of Luther's *Sämmtliche Werke* was Walch, who published
them 1740-1753. They form volume XXII of his edition.
He gives an account of how they were collected, and a discussion of their value in his preface. His labors were confined to comparing Aurifaber, Stangwald and Selneccer, as
none of the sources were then known.[2]

The so-called Stuttgart-Leipzig edition of 1836 is a
mere reprint of Walch.

A new edition, on exactly the same plan was undertaken
in 1844 by K. E. Förstemann. It was based like Walch on
a comparison of Aurifaber, Stangwald and Selneccer.
Förstemann died when three volumes of this work had been
completed, and H. E. Bindseil edited the fourth and last.
In his preface to this he states the method of his work. He
compared not only the three editions and Walch, but also
Luther's letters, and in part the Latin edition (in the MS.

---

[1] Irmischer, *op. cit.*, vol. 57, p. xiv. Förstemann-Bindseil, *op. cit*, vol.
iv, Einl., xxxvii. Some of Selneccer's minute changes are given here.
They are simply verbal.

[2] See *infra*, Appendix.

he edited later). He discussed the sources with more science than any one had used hitherto, though he knew nothing of them except as they were mentioned in Aurifaber's preface and Mathesius' sermons. He went as far as any one could who had to rely on the old collections, and who did not know the sources directly.

In 1854 Irmischer edited the *Tischreden* for the *Sämmtliche Werke*, published at Frankfurt-am-Main and Erlangen, of which they form six volumes numbered 57 to 62. Irmischer proceeded on the same critical principles as Walch, although they had really been exhausted by previous editors. Since then no other work of this kind has been undertaken. The volume of the Weimar edition which is to be dedicated to the *Tischreden* will be edited on entirely different principles.[1]

The years 1864-1866 saw a new Latin edition of the Table Talk—the first since Rebenstock's. Bindseil edited it from a MS. he found in the Library of the Orphan Asylum at Halle. He rightly assigned the collection of *Tischreden* found therein to Lauterbach, but was sorely puzzled to explain the relations of his MS. with Rebenstock on the one hand and Aurifaber on the other.[2] He did the work of editing thoroughly, pointing out the parallels in the German and previous Latin editions.

The year 1872 marks an era in the publication of the *Tischreden*. Prior to this time the labors of editors had been confined to working over and over the old collections, especially Aurifaber's. Beginning with the printing of Lauterbach's *Tagebuch* in 1872 the efforts of scholars have been turned to the fresher and far more fruitful field of

---

[1] *Cf. infra*, p. 54, n. 1.

[2] He merely stated the problem without answering it. The answer was, as we have seen, given by Meyer.

the original notes. J. K. Seidemann [1] was the first to see their value, and he edited the best of the sources in the *Tagebuch* mentioned above. He prepared two other MSS. for the press, Dietrich's notebook, which has never been printed, since Seidemann's unfortunate death interrupted his useful labors, and the *Analecta* which were later published by Lösche, both men believing them to have been the Mathesian collection. The value of the *Tagebuch* was immediately recognized by scholars, who saw the relative worthlessness of the older collections of *Tischreden*. Unfortunately Seidemann's work on Dietrich, the most valuable source now unpublished, has never been taken up again. Seidemann's " diplomatically correct copy " was used by Köstlin in his great work.

In 1885 Wrampelmeyer followed with Cordatus's *Tagebuch*. In the absence of the means of judging it which we possess now, he immensely overrated its value; to him even its faults were qualities, proving its authenticity. Some of its failings were pointed out by Preger in his edition of Schlaginhaufen, some by Kroker in his *Mathesian Collection*.

Schlaginhaufen's notes found an able editor in 1888 in the person of Preger. They at once took their place as among the best of the sources, ranking along with Lauterbach's *Tagebuch* and Dietrich's notes.

In 1892 Lösche edited a rather worthless MS. under the title *Analecta Lutherana et Melanchthonia,* believing it to be the Mathesian collection, the existence of which had long been known by references to it by Aurifaber and Mathesius himself. Lösche was lead to this task by his interest in

---

[1] Lösche gives a sketch of Seidemann's labors in this field. *Analecta,* Einl., p. 1 *et seq.;* Köstlin, *op. cit.* (ed. 1889). Vorwort, p. iii, says he used Dietrich in Seidemann's copy.

Mathesius, whose life he had written and whose works he had edited. Seidemann had left a correct copy of the MS. and pointed out a large number of parallels in the sources. In verifying his parallels Lösche found three hundred which had been overlooked by Seidemann. A later authority found that Lösche had himself overlooked several hundred.[1] We have already seen that the MS. was the copy of a copy of Mathesius' notebook of 1540. Lösche proved this date and also that the MS. dated from the last part of the 15th century, probably after Mathesius's death in 1565.

The real Mathesian collection was edited in 1903 by Kroker. It is extremely valuable as opening up new sources in a reliable copy.

One attempt, and only one, has hitherto been made to get a comprehensive edition of the *Tischreden* founded on the sources. This was undertaken by Professor A. F. Hoppe, of St. Louis in the reprint of Walch's *Sämmtliche Werke*. under the auspices of the Lutherischer Concordia Verlag, 1887. The scope of the edition is indicated in its title *Dr. Martin Luthers Colloquia oder Tischreden; zum ersten Male berichtigt und erneuert durch Uebersetzung der beiden Hauptquellen der Tischreden aus der lateinischen Originalen, nämlich des Tagebuchs des Dr. Conrad Cordatus über Luther 1537 und des Tagebuchs des M. Anto. Lauterbach auf das Jahr 1538.*

In his introduction Professor Hoppe gives a very just idea of the worthlessness of the old editions, which are nothing but Aurifaber printed over and over again. Indeed Aurifaber is very severely treated by the new editor who says he handled the originals very arbitrarily, took sayings out of their context, made mistakes in reading, in dates, in translation, in assigning sayings to wrong per-

---

[1] Lösche, *op. cit.*, Einl., p. 6; Kroker, *loc. cit.*, Einl., p. 28, note 4.

sons, in short falsified and altered to suit himself. A glowing description of the high worth of the two sources used is given, taken from the introductions of their editors, and then the work of this new edition is described. 520 duplicates, found either twice in the *Tischreden*, or elsewhere in the works, are eliminated. The 1843 paragraphs of Cordatus and the 488 paragraphs of Lauterbach are translated and incorporated. Twenty-four bits from *Khumer* (*i. e.* the material printed in Lauterbach's *Tagebuch* by Seidemann) are also used. The Bible quotations have been improved by reference to that book. Sayings which are separated in Walch are joined, and others which are wrongly joined are separated.

The order in Walch has been maintained, *i. e.* the topical order of Aurifaber. Whenever a parallel to one of his sayings has been found in the sources, the account is corrected in accordance with the sources or their account substituted. The parallels so treated form but a small part (perhaps one-tenth) of the whole edition; all sayings which have no parallels are reprinted exactly as before, except the duplicates which are taken out. A large number of sayings in Lauterbach and Cordatus which have no parallels in Walch are printed in Appendices.[1]

The result is disappointing. This is partly because the edition came out before the other sources were known, partly from too great conservatism of treatment. The bulk of the work is the same, after all, as that in Walch. The material from Cordatus and Lauterbach is thrown in promiscuously in the old order, which makes it less accessible and less valuable than in the original form. The estimate of Cordatus by Wrampelmeyer is taken at its face value, and most of his material which we know to be value-

---

[1] Hoppe, *op. cit.*, Einl., *in fine*.

less is inserted as an improvement on Aurifaber. It is singular that the editor does not recognize (what he must have known) that there were other *Hauptquellen*, and that if Aurifaber is worthless when we can find a parallel to him in Lauterbach, he must have been so in other cases.

The editors of the Weimar edition[1] plan to dedicate one of their last volumes to the Table Talk, basing it on a critical study of the sources. This will certainly be the most satisfactory of all the editions; indeed, unless further sources are discovered, which is not probable, it should be definitive. Let us see what may be hoped from such an edition—a convenient way of summing up the results of our researches in the sources.

In the first place the original notes should be the only authority used, including among them the notebooks which have survived in the Mathesian collection, but excluding the collections of Lauterbach and Aurifaber as too unreliable.

The notebooks should be used with discrimination. Those of Dietrich, Schlaginhaufen, Lauterbach, and Mathesius, are *prima facie* reliable; the others should be used rather as checks on these and as helps in textual criticism than for their own independent value, which is slight.

The MSS. should all be carefully collated, in order to get the best text. To do this all parallels must be noted, both for the sake of the text and for the dates which are indispensable to a really scientific edition. Parallels must,

---

[1] Professor Drescher, of Breslau, the editor of the Weimar edition, has kindly informed me, through the publishing house of Hermann Böhlaus Nachfolger, that the last volume is to be assigned to the *Tischreden*, which will come next after the letters, on which work has already been begun.

of course, be carefully divided into true, apparent, and derived, and treated accordingly.[1]

The chronological order should be preserved. The topical was more useful to those whose first purpose was an exposition of doctrine or an authoritative statement in some problem of theology, but for the scientific historian, as well as for the ordinary reader to-day, the chronological order is readily seen to be the best. The source of each saying should be indicated.

An edition on this plan would have a real use. It would save the scholar going to a number of sources and reading over much of material which is often repetitious. By getting it all together it would throw a much stronger light on the development of Luther's life and thought than the fragmentary sources do.

Let us see how much time we can expect to be fairly covered by the original notes.

1531-1533. The notes of Schlaginhaufen can be dated with considerable accuracy, and run from November, 1531 to September, 1532. The notes of Dietrich, which he dates on his title-page 1529-1535 really fall, with very few exceptions between November, 1531 and October, 1533. Their order has been restored and their chronology established by Preger.[2]

1536-1537. Notes of Lauterbach and Weller in 6th section of Mathesius. Fuller parallels and supplementary material found in the MS. known as *Colloquia Serotina*.

1538. Lauterbach's *Tagebuch*, edited by Seidemann.

---

[1] *True* parallels being those in which two or more reporters took down the same saying; *apparent* parallels those in which the similarity is due to Luther's having repeated the same story more than once; and *derived* parallels those which are due to copying.

[2] Preger, *op. cit.*, Einl., p. xxi *et seq*. See *supra*, p. 42.

1539. Copies from Lauterbach's *Tagebuch* in 5th section of Mathesius.

1540. Notes of Mathesius in his collection. 1st section of Kroker's edition.

1542-1543. Notes of Heydenreich in 2d section of Mathesius.

1544. Notes of Besold in 3d section of Mathesius.

We must notice that the sources given above show different degrees of accuracy in dating. Lauterbach's *Tagebuch of 1538* gives the day on which everything was said; in other cases our work has to proceed from internal evidence, which gives sometimes the exact date, often only an approximate date. *E. g.* we can say that no. 377 in Schlaginhaufen was said May 31, 1532, but we can only say that nos. 378-548 fell between June and September of that year. By a sort of system of interpolation we can get the date more nearly; the chances are that a number at the beginning of this series fell in June, one in the middle in July or August, and one near the end in September. These dates are sufficiently accurate to give the basis of a chronological order of *Tischreden*. They will become more and more accurate as more is found out about Luther's life, and as parallels from other notebooks, and circumstances gathered from the letters and other documents are compared with them.

Secondly, we must observe that quite a number of notes can be found outside of these years and the sources indicated for them which will partly supply the lacunae. Some of those in Cordatus can be dated; a few other dates are given in Dietrich, others in the fourth section of the Mathesian collection. Great caution should be used in the insertion of such notes; isolated sayings in an unchronological source should not be given the same weight as those which have, so to speak, a strong presumptive case from the fact

that they stand in a source which arranges its notes chronologically. Still, with care, many notes can be rescued from
the sources which will partly fill up the blank spaces.

For the early thirties Dietrich, Schlaginhaufen and Cordatus are the sources. By collation of the three much may
be gained. We often find little groups of chronologically
ordered sayings which supply and complement each other
What cannot be got into chronological order should be put
into an appendix labelled, Sayings prior to 1537 from Cordatus, Dietrich and Schlaginhaufen.[1]

The notes from 1536-1540 can be dated with great accuracy, and leave little to be desired. They are also full.

It is for the last years of Luther's life that the chronology of the notes is hardest to determine. Those of
Heydenreich are rather uncertain, sparse, and known only
in a copy. Those of Plato are altogether unreliable, being
mainly extracts from others. Those of Stolz and Aurifaber have become irrecoverably lost in the collection of the
latter. Those sayings which cannot be dated must be rele-
gated to an appendix. The smaller their number is the
nearer will the edition reach the desired goal.

Such an edition would do away with the doubt and hesi-
tation with which we now have to read the Table Talk.
Any one who has carefully examined the best sources will
surely feel that we must give them the same degree of con-
fidence at least that we give to Luther's sermons; and in
a source of Luther's life so rich in material, such an in-
crease in certainty will be an immense gain.

The source of each saying should be indicated, as a
means of judging of its worth. In summing up we may
say that the greatest faith can be placed in Lauterbach, Dietrich and Schlaginhaufen, and only a little less in Mathesius,

[1] Cf. Kroker, op. cit., p. 63.

Besold and Heydenreich. Cordatus, Weller and Plato are untrustworthy, but with discrimination much of value may be abstracted from them. The collections of Lauterbach and Aurifaber are practically useless. The more we compare them with the originals, the deeper they sink in our estimation. But a complete edition would have to take from them all that could not be found in better form somewhere else, printing it as so much new material, inferior in value to the sources, but not negligible.[1]

[1] *Cf.* Kroker, *op. cit.*, pp. 64, 65; Meyer, *loc. cit.*, p. 36.

CHAPTER VII

The Translations

THERE have been two principal translations of the *Tischreden* into English, and a number of minor ones. The first,[1] made by Captain Henry Bell, was printed at London in 1652. The Translator's Preface is interesting. It begins:

I, Captain Henry Bell, do hereby declare, both to the present age and also to posterity, that being employed beyond the seas in state affairs years together, both by King James and also by the late King Charles, in Germany, I did hear and understand, in all places, great bewailing and lamentation made, by reason of the destroying and burning above fourscore thousand of Martin Luther's books, entitled, *His Last Divine Discourses*...

This book did so forward the Reformation, that the Pope then living, *viz.*, Gregory XIII, understanding what great hurt

---

[1] *Colloquia Mensalia; or, Familiar Discourses of Dr. Martin Luther, at his Table, which in his Lifetime he held with divers Learned Men, such as were Philip Melanchthon, Casparus Cruciger, Justus Jonas, Paulus Eberus, Vitus Dietericus, Johannes Bugenhagen, Johannes Forsterus, and Others. Containing Questions and Answers Touching Religion and other main points of Doctrine; as also Many Notable Histories, and all sorts of Learning, Comforts, Advices, Prophecies, Admonitions, Directions, Instructions, Collected first together by Dr. Antonius Lauterbach, and afterwards disposed into certain Commonplaces by Dr. John Aurifaber, D. D.* This title is followed by six quotations as to the utility of *sacra ad mensam*. A very learned "Epistle Dedicatorie to the Right Honorable John Kendrick, Lord Major, The Right Worshipful the Sheriffs and Aldermen, the Common Council, and other Worthie Senators and Citizens of the famous Citie of London," signed by Thomas Thorowgood, is then inserted.

and prejudice he and his popish religion had already received, by reason of the said Luther's Divine Discourses, and also fearing the same might bring further contempt and mischief upon himself, and upon the Popish Church, he, therefore, to prevent the same, did fiercely stir up and instigate the Emperor then in being, *viz.*, Rudolphus II, to make an edict throughout the whole Empire, that all the aforesaid printed books should be burnt. . . . . . which edict was speedily put into execution accordingly.

It pleased God, however, that in 1626 one of Bell's German friends should find one of the aforesaid printed books in a deep obscure hole, and being afraid to keep it, because Ferdinand II was a severe persecutor of the Protestant Religion, and at the same time calling to mind that Bell " had the High Dutch Tongue very perfect," sent it to him to translate into English.

Bell was warned by a vision that he should translate it, and shortly after he was committed to the Keeper of Gate-House, Westminster, on a warrant which was not shown him, and kept there in prison ten whole years, the first five of which he spent translating the book.

" Then after I had finished the said translation in prison, the late archbishop of Canterbury, Dr. Laud, understanding that I had translated such a book, called Martin Luther's Divine Discourses, sent unto me his chaplain Dr. Bray " to request the perusal of the book. After some demur Bell sent the book which Laud kept two years and then returned under fear that the Commons would call him to account.

And presently, when I was set at liberty by warrant from the whole house of Lords, according to his majesty's direction in that behalf; but shortly afterwards the archbishop fell into his troubles, and was by the parliament sent unto the Tower, and afterwards beheaded. Insomuch that I could never since hear anything touching the printing of my book.

The House of Commons having then notice that I had translated the aforesaid book, they sent for me, and did appoint a committee to see it, and the translation, and diligently to enquire whether the translation did agree with the original or no; whereupon they desired me to bring the same before them, sitting then in the Treasury Chamber. And Sir Edward Dearing being chairman, said unto me, that he was acquainted with a learned minister beneficed in Essex, who had lived long in England, but was born in High Germany, in the Palatinate, named Mr. Paul Amiraut, whom the committee sending for, desired him to take both the original and translation into his custody, and diligently to compare them together, and to make report unto the said committee whether he found that I had rightly and truly translated it according to the original; which report he made accordingly, and they being satisfied therein, referred it to two of the assembly, Mr. Charles Herle and Mr. Edward Corbet, desiring them diligently to peruse the same, and to make report unto them if they thought it fitting to be printed and published.

Whereupon they made report, dated the 10th of November, 1646, that they found it to be an excellent divine work, worthy the light and publishing, especially in regard that Luther, in the said Discourses, did revoke his opinion, which he formerly held, touching Consubstantiation in the Sacrament. Whereupon the House of Commons, the 24th of February, 1646, did give order for the printing thereof.

Given under my hand the third day of July, 1650.

HENRY BELL.

This account is such a tissue of mistakes and improbabilities that it is hardly worth serious criticism. It is clear both from the absence of all other evidence, and the large number of early editions of Luther's *Tischreden* which have come down to us, that no such order was ever issued by Rudolph II as that which Bell describes. The ten years' arbitrary imprisonment is so improbable that it may be dismissed.[1] The whole thing has the air of being invented to heighten the interest of the translation; even the vision of the old man does not seem to be a genuine bit of self-deception.

The introduction is followed by the Report of the Committee of the House of Commons, which gives an interesting

Testimonie and Judgment: Wee finde many excellent divine things are conteined in the Book worthie the light and publick view. Amongst which, Luther professeth that he acknowledgeth his error which hee formerly held touching the real presence *corporaliter in Coena Domini.*

But wee finde withal many impertinent things: som things which will require a grain or two of Salt, and som things which will require a Marginal note or a Preface.

A " Marginal note " is herewith added by the Committee:

And no marvel, that among so much serious discourse in matters of religion, sometimes at Table som impertinent things might intermix themselves and som things *liberius dicta* to recreate and refresh the Companie.

Then comes the order of the Commons to print it, and then a short extract from Aurifaber called " Testimonie of

---

[1] Arbitrary imprisonment was resorted to at this time, but only in important political cases, such as those of Pym and Eliot. It is possible that Bell may have been really imprisoned for some cause he prefers not to mention. Hazlitt says in a note that the cause was that he pressed for the payment of arrears in his salary, an explanation for which he gives no authority.

This Preface worried Walch (*op. cit.,* vol. xxii, Einl., pp. 17, 18) a good deal. He had not seen the original, but quotes from a partial translation of J. Beaumont, whose interest in it was due to the supernatural phenomenon recounted. (*Tractat von Geistern, Erscheinungen,* &c., iii, 73.)

Aurifaber in his Preface to his Book" and notes from "W.D.", "J.L." and "J.D.". Then Aurifaber's preface, dated 1569, in full.

The same Eighty Chapters are here as in Aurifaber, but the order is somewhat changed. The XIXth Caption is changed from "Vom Sacrament des Alters des waren Leibs und Bluts Christi" to "Of the sacrament of the Lord's Supper."

There is an appendix of Luther's Prophecies. The Imprimatur, at the end, is dated August, 1650, signed by John Downame.

Comparison shows that this was translated from one of Aurifaber's editions; it is nearest like that of 1571 (See Appendix p. 121).[1] The translation is not complete, a very rough guess would be that two-thirds of the original was translated. The omissions were made with the purpose of pleasing the theologians of that day and place. Much of the chapter on The Sacrament is omitted, but I can find nothing in it to justify the Committee's opinion that Luther retracted his former error on this point.[2]

This translation was reprinted 1791 with "The Life and Character of Dr. Martin Luther: by John Gottlieb Burckhardt, D. D., minister of the German Lutheran Congregation at the Savoy, in London" prefixed. In this edition, between pages iv and v of Bell's narrative there is a "Picture of Popery" by John Ryland in four pages. It is in the good old-fashioned style of invective. In this

[1] Points of resemblance are: Mention of Lauterbach's and Aurifaber's name on titlepage; date of preface 1569; Prophecies at the end, and others less striking.

[2] Bell himself implies the Committee had *told him* that Luther had retracted on this point. Walch, *op. cit.*, vol. xxii, p. 18, speaks of the charge and indignantly denies it.

edition the chapter on Witchcraft was left out, as well as the Report of the Committee of the Commons, and the Dedicatory Epistle and Testimonies. This translation was reprinted again in 1818.

Another partial translation, *Choice Fragments from the Discourses of Luther,* was published in 1832. The translator, who does not give his name, was a zealous Protestant and a decorous, conventional Englishman. He suppressed with the greatest care whatever really showed the free, joyous and somewhat coarse character of Luther, and in his translation we see him transformed into an English clergyman with an unctuous regard for the proprieties, polished, well brought up, grave and formal in his conversation.[1]

The *Tischreden* were translated a third time by William Hazlitt, son of the celebrated essayist, in 1848. The preface is taken half from Bell's narrative, which is quoted without comment in an abridged form, and half from the preface to Brunet's French translation, adding to the errors of the sources several of the author's own. He does not acknowledge his indebtedness to Brunet, but follows him in calling " Selneccer " " Selneuer " and in giving Stangwald's edition of 1591 as of 1590. From Brunet he quotes Fabricius, *Centifolium Lutheranum,* as though he had seen the book himself. From Brunet he gets the anecdote of Luther's throwing the gruel into his disciple's face, but he adds without any authority whatever that it was "told by Luther himself to Dr. Zincgreff " (who was born

---

[1] This translation is in the Lenox Library. My characterization is taken from Brunet, *Propos de Table*, Introduction, p. 18: " Il a supprimé avec le plus grand soin tout ce qui montre dans son interieur le père de la réforme; il a voulu le peindre en beau; il en fait un prébendier anglicain, poli, bien élevé, à la parole grave," etc.

half a century after Luther's death).[1] A translation of
Aurifaber's preface is given, but only a selection of the *Tischreden*, embracing perhaps a fourth of the material found
in Aurifaber. The style of the English is excellent, colloquial and yet smooth. It seems to have been made from
the German (though Hazlitt tells us he had compared the
translations of Michelet with his own) and is sufficiently
accurate.[2]

This work has reappeared a number of times. Others
of minor importance have been made, among which
may be mentioned a number of books either translated from
Michelet's *Vie de Martin Luther par lui-même* or closely
modelled on it. Hazlitt Englished this work, others pub-

---

[1] Hazlitt, *Luther's Table Talk*, Introduction, p. 10 (ed. of 1848):
"An anecdote told by Luther himself to Dr. Zincgreff, amusingly illus-
trates the assiduity of these German Boswells. During a colloquy, in
which Dominus Martinus was exhibiting his wonted energy and vivacity,
he observed a disciple hard at work with pencil and paper. The Doctor,
slily filling his huge wooden spoon with the gruel he was discussing by
way of supper, rose, and going to the absorbed note-taker, threw the
gruel in his face, and said, laughing lustily: ' Put that down too!'"
Hazlitt gives no authority for this story, which he probably took from
a footnote in Brunet's Introduction, but I have found it in Dr. J. W.
Zincgreff's *Teutscher Nation Apophthegmata*, p. 252, where it is in the
following form: "Als er [*sc.* Luther] eines jungen Studenten eines
rechten Speichelleckers beym Tisch gewahr wurde, dir hinder ihm
stund und alles was er redte ohn verstand oder unterscheid in seine
Schreibtafel aufgezeichnete, verdrosse ihm sehr, liess mit Fleiss einen
gruëltzen drüber und Sagte: 'Schreib diesen auch auf!'" Zincgreff
gives no authority. I have not been able to find the story in the *Tischreden* or any of Luther's works, and it has no intrinsic probability. We
have no other instance of Luther indulging in a practical joke. The
story is quoted literally and without remark by Brunet. It is Hazlitt
who is responsible for the addition that Luther himself told it to Zincgreff, which is impossible, as the latter was born in 1591. Besides
noticing the lack of critical discernment, it is interesting to see how the
anecdote grew in Hazlitt's translation.

[2] In his translation of Michelet's book referred to just below, he says
he compared Bell's, Michelet's, Audin's, and his own.

lished books with the same title either with or without acknowledgment of the source.[1]

A considerable number of Luther's sayings are translated into French by the celebrated historian Jules Michelet in a book entitled *Mémoires de Luther écrits par lui-même;* traduits et mis en ordre par M. Michelet . . . . Paris, 1835. The author's preface testifies to his admiration of the reformer, although he is not a Protestant. The work consists of extracts from Luther's writings and Table Talk *passim.* Bk., IV, however, consists entirely of extracts from the Table Talk, to illustrate Luther's family life, and opinions about marriage, children, nature and the Bible, the Fathers, schoolmen, Pope, councils, universities, arts, music and preaching. The chapter ends with Luther's admission of his own violence and a rather feeble translation of the passage in which Luther says he must have patience with the Pope and Käthe. The appendix (p. xci) describes Aurifaber's edition of the *Tischreden.*[2]

The first (and perhaps the only) attempt to translate a considerable portion of the *Tischreden* into French in a volume by themselves, was made by Gustave Brunet: *Les Propos de Table de Martin Luther, revus sur les éditions originales et traduites pour la première fois en français.* Paris, 1844. The introduction is bright, but uncritical. After an eloquent appreciation of the value of the Table Talk and an apology for its occasional coarseness, the author tells us how the sayings were collected, repeating the

---

[1] Full list of these in Appendix.

[2] From which we may infer that it was used. Other *Tischreden* appeared in French in J. M. V. Audin: *Histoire de la vie, des ouvrages et des doctrines de Luther,* 1839. These are spoken of by Hazlitt (*supra,* note 1). Audin was a Catholic historian. The work is in the Astor Library.

anecdote of Zincgreff, but without any reference except the name. A short account of the work of Michelet and Audin is followed by an equally brief description of the German editions, in which the same mistakes are made as were made four years later by Hazlitt, who probably copied from him. Selneccer appears as Selneuer, the edition of 1591 appears as 1590, and the first volume of Rebenstock is assigned to 1558, an error not corrected in any account until Bindseil's *Colloquia* appeared, in 1863. An account is given of the English translation of Bell, and of that of 1832.

The translator claims to have compared the editions and to have selected the best text. He changed the order of the other editions entirely, writing solely from the point of view of interest. His principle of selection is the opposite of that of Hazlitt, the more spicy a thing is the more relish it has for him. His copious notes make the work more readable. He begins with a chapter on " Le diable, les sorcières, les incubes &c." This is followed by one entitled " Contes, apologues et joyeux devis." The worst of these he inserts in the notes in Latin, remarking " qu'ils ont tout l'air d'une page des facéties de Pogge ou des nouvelles de Morlino." Next to the " petits contes polissons " the author likes best those in which Luther talked about his enemies, or showed himself the victim of some superstition.

CHAPTER VIII

The Table Talk in Literature

The period of the Reformation in Germany was one of great literary as well as great spiritual activity. Not since the efflorescence of lyric and epic poetry in the thirteenth century, nor again until the latter part of the eighteenth, do we find anything equal in quantity and power to the literary output of this great age. True, no world poet appeared who contends the palm with Goethe and Schiller or even with Gottfried von Strassburg and Walther von der Vogelweide: "the Aristophanic age produced no Aristophanes,"[1] but nevertheless the literature of the Reformation is full of significance, vitality and charm.

The characteristics of the time were intense nationalism, strong religious feeling, and a powerful appeal to the common man, in fact intensity in all forms, which often showed itself in bitter satire and mocking laughter. The title of Pauli's farcical stories, *Schimpf und Ernst*—mocking jest and earnest mingled, might well be the motto of the age. Here, as in the tales of Claus Narr, the romances, the plays, many of them, of Hans Sachs, and the fable of *Reinecke Fuchs* and those attributed to Aesop, we see the appeal to the peasant, the common man, over against the old aristocracy. Sometimes the appeal was not to the peasant's best side—the adventures of Till Eulenspiegel show how a clever

[1] Scherer, *Geschichte d. deut. Literatur.*

scamp outwits his superiors, and the apotheosis of coarseness in St. Grobianus, a character invented by Brandt in his famous satire the *Ship of Fools,* was typical of the least pleasant side of the exuberant vitality which made itself manifest everywhere.[1]

The fiery dialogues of Hutton, as well as the appeals of Luther and a host of less famous men, show how deeply rooted was the nationalism which rebelled against the crafty domination of foreigners; but deepest and loudest of all was the cry for a purer religion and a more vital faith. The satirization of the clergy had been common since the time of Walther von der Vogelweide at least, but the number and bitterness of these satires increased in the sixteenth century. The polished wit of Erasmus supplied to the upper class who could appreciate his Latin style what the *Litterae Obscurorum Virorum* of Rubianus and his collaborators gave to the students, and such popular *Pasquille* as *Die Krankheit der Messe* and *Der Curtisan und Pfründenfresser* furnished to those who could read only German.

Of this wonderful time Luther was the heart and soul. How tremendous was the place he filled in the hearts of his countrymen may be seen by the popularity of his works, as well as by the frequency of literary allusion to him. The press was full of such little pamphlets as *Luther's Passion,* and even the plays were deeply influenced by his teaching.[2] None of Luther's works was more popular than his Table Talk, published, as we have seen, by Aurifaber, in 1566. Before the century was over no less than twelve

---

[1] Dedekind, in 1549, wrote a poem on St. Grobianus, who is always appearing elsewhere. The same spirit is seen in Fischer's translation of Rabelais.

[2] Very many such pamphlets are reproduced in O. Schade's *Satiren und Pasquille aus der Reformationzeit.* For the influence on the drama, see below on the Franckfurt *Faust.*

editions were called for in German, besides the Latin translation.[1]

The cause of their popularity is not hard to discover. In reading them we have the concentrated spirit of the sixteenth century, the love of anecdote and satire, the popular note, the strong national and religious feeling, and even the flavor of "grobianism" which nothing escaped. Besides all this, there is the personal interest, which is perhaps the chief one to-day, and was not less powerful then; the same sort of interest which will always make Eckermann's *Gespräche mit Goethe*, or Bourienne's *Mémoires* of Napoleon widely read. We see the great man's daily life and intimate thoughts portrayed with a frankness and unreserve which are refreshing.

In reading the Table Talk we are constantly reminded of the dialogues and satires so common and so popular at that time. Occasional allusions to Grobianus, the frequent appearance of stories about animals, and the perpetual invective against Rome and the clergy,—all these are revelations of the *Zeitgeist* which appears in all the literary productions of the time.[2] Luther, however, not only borrowed much from his contemporaries, but greatly enriched their speech in return. Even his casual utterances often impressed themselves on the speech of his countrymen, and attained a proverbial currency. Such sayings as:

[1] See Appendix for these editions. The popularity of the work seems to have borne some relation to the general literary activity of the country; there were only four editions in the seventeenth century, two in the eighteenth, and more than nine in the nineteenth, not counting five editions of sources.

[2] For Grobianus, *cf.* Wrampelmeyer, *op. cit.*, no. 1738. *Cf.* Luther's animal fables, *e, g.*, Seidemann, *op. cit.*, p. 114, *et saepe*, with such satires as, "Ein Gesprech eines Fuchs und Wolfs," in Schade, *op. cit.*, vol. ii, no. iii. *Cf.* also *ibid.*, vol. i, no. i: "Ein Clag und Bitt der deutschen Nation," with such of Luther's sayings as Seidemann, *op. cit.*, p. 10.

Frühe aufstehen und jung freien
Soll niemands gereuen,[1]

and

Wer will haben rein sein haus
Der behalt Pfaffen und Mönche draus,[2]

are good examples. Some sayings found in his conversation
have been such as he disapproved and refuted, though even
thus they took a lasting form in the way he quoted them.
Such, for example is the:

Bleibe gern allein,
So bleiben euer Herzen rein.[3]

Perhaps the most famous of his authentic sayings is one
which is thoroughly characteristic of the apostle of marriage and the domestic virtues as against the Catholic ideal
of celibacy:

[1] Xanthippus: "Gute alte deutsche Sprüche," in *Preussische Jahrbücher*, vol. 85 (July to Sept., 1896), three articles, pp. 149, 344, and
503 respectively. This saying is on p. 351, quoted from Förstemann-
Bindseil, *op. cit.*, vol. iv, p. 41.

[2] *Ibid.*, p. 363, quoting Förstemann-Bindseil, *op. cit.*, vol. ii, p. 407.

[3] *Ibid.*, p. 151, quoting Förstemann-Bindseil, *op. cit.*, vol. iii, p. 164.
Other examples are given elsewhere, *e. g.*, p. 505. Zincgreff, in his
Teutscher Nation Apophthegmata, gives some proverbs of Luther, which
appear to be mainly apocryphal. Like other great men, Luther had sayings fathered upon him which were not genuine. Such is the celebrated

"Wer liebt nicht Wein, Weib und Gesang,
Der bleibt ein Narr sein Lebenslang."

It is not found in any of Luther's works, nor in the *Table Talk*, and
was first printed, as far as known, in 1775, in *Wandsbecker Boten*. Cf.
Köstlin, *op. cit.*, vol. ii, p. 678, note to p. 507. The verse has just
enough of Luther's spirit to make it a good caricature.

Nicht liebers auf Erden
Denn Frawenlieb wems kann werden.[1]

A still profounder influence is seen in the coloring taken from the *Tischreden* by the *Faust* written anonymously and produced at Frankfurt in 1587. This, of course, is doubly interesting as bringing the work into a direct relation with the greatest masterpiece of German literature. In this play Mephistopheles "takes many sententious rimes from Brandt's *Narrenschiff* and Luther's *Tischreden.*"[2] The author makes Faust's fall from grace an apostasy from the Wittenberg theology, and his repentence is taken from expressions of Luther's in the Table Talk.

The brilliant literary promise of the sixteenth century was sadly disappointed in the seventeenth and early eighteenth. It really seemed as if the Thirty Years' War had blasted all the artistic powers which were so strongly developed before it. The nation looked to France for its literature and canons of taste, and the Table Talk fell into the obscurity which most German works shared in this period. Something of a revival is seen in the renewed in-

---

[1] Förstemann-Bindseil, *op. cit.*, vol. iv, pp. 75, Xanthippus, *loc. cit.*, p. 346. The enemies of Luther have twisted this into a confession of sensuality. The same idea of Luther as an apostle of the joys of the flesh is exhibited by one who was no enemy of his, the once celebrated Philarète Chasle, in an article called "La Renaissance Sensuelle,' in *Revue des Deux Mondes*, March, 1842, where he compares him to Rabelais, Skelton and Folengo.

[2] Schmidt: "Faust und Luther," in *Sitzungsberichte d. k. Preuss. Akad. d. Wiss.* The author collects a large number of parallel passages which show how much *Faust* was influenced by the *Tischreden.* Minor points are that the devil appears to Faust as he had to Luther; Helena is modelled on Luther's idea of a *succubus;* Faust's impression of Rome is taken from Luther's words on the same, and also his estimate of the " frankly swinish " life of the Turks. See especially pp. 568, 571.

terest taken in it in the nineteenth century, not only in Germany [1] but in other countries as well.[2]

We have spoken of those qualities of the *Tischreden* which are due to its environment and make it interesting as a typical product of the age; let us now turn to some of its individual peculiarities.

In the first place the Table Talk is not a literary work, in the narrow sense of that term, at all. In an age of roughness and bad literary form it has not even the polish of Luther's written works, or of the dialogues or plays with which we have been comparing it. The first thing which strikes us on opening one of the sources (not Aurifaber) is the mixture of languages spoken by the company. Latin and German are so easily interchangeable that a sentence is often begun in one and ended in the other. " Christus is unzuverstehen, quia est deus ";[3] " Mein ganz Leben ist eitel patientia." [4] It is almost superfluous to give examples of so common a phenomenon.

The reason of this was simply that both languages were

---

[1] An unfavorable estimate of the Table Talk, together with the idea that it had a strong influence in fixing the German bürger type, is found in Lavisse & Rambaud, *Histoire Générale*, iv, p. 423. The number of editions (see *supra*, p. 69, n. 2) shows their popularity.

[2] For translations, see Appendix. Brunet (*Propos de Table*, Introduction) says that Bayle commented on them. See Hereford, *Literary Relations of England and Germany in the Sixteenth Century.*

[3] Preger, *op. cit.*, no. 301.

[4] Bindseil, *Colloquia*, vol. iii, p. 167. That this was their ordinary method of talking can be seen not only from the Table Talk, but from the testimony of Jonas, who tells us (Letter of July 6, 1537, quoted by Meyer, *loc. cit.*, p. 4) that he found Luther sick in bed " nunc Deum Patrem nunc Christum Dominum, nunc Latine nunc Germanice invocantem." This mixture, which we call *macaronic*, and the Germans *messingisch* (Kroker, *op. cit.*, p. 5), would have appeared less strange even in a literary work at that time. Among numerous examples of it I will cite only the well-known *Carmina Burana*.

equally familiar, and the attempt to discover any other reason is unnecessary. Wrampelmeyer [1] is led by his patriot-
ism to the discovery that German is the language used to
express the main thought, an idea which seems to me fanci-
ful. Lösche thinks Latin was used largely to spare the
women's ears what they should not hear. [2] This is a nine-
teenth-century idea, which would be entirely alien to the
sixteenth. The precaution would have been useless, for
Käthe, at least, knew enough Latin to keep up with the
conversation. [3] Then again Luther took no pains to avoid
remarks to or about her which shock our fastidious de-
corum, though they certainly would not have appeared ob-
jectionable to the most cultivated taste of Luther's time. [4]

In general the students put down the sayings in the language in which they were uttered, as would usually be the
easier thing to do, but sometimes they translated a German
remark into Latin which they could write faster. For the
same reason they would put all their own remarks in that
tongue, and all matter supplied by them, such as details
of time, place, and occasion. One instance in which they
clearly translated Luther's remarks is that in which he is
represented as consoling his poor old dying Muhme Lehna
in the learned tongue which must have been unfamiliar to
her. [5] Sometimes Greek [6] and even Hebrew are introduced,

[1] Wrampelmeyer, *op. cit.*, Einl., p. 34.

[2] Lösche, *Analecta*, Einl., p. 3.   [3] Kroker, *op. cit.*, no. 3.

[4] E. g., Wrampelmeyer, *op. cit.*, no. 1597; Preger, *op. cit.*, no. 419.

[5] Bindseil, *op. cit.*, vol. iii, p. 217. *Cf. ibid.*, p. 213, where he consoles
Cranach in the same tongue.

[6] Kroker, *op. cit.*, no. 3. An example of the use of Hebrew is found
in the introduction of the word *Scheflimini* (*Shebh l'mini*, quoted from
Psalm cx. 1) in Kroker, *op. cit.*, no. 242 (and thence taken into Aurifaber, Förstemann-Bindseil, *op. cit.*, vol. i, p. 322) without any indication, to the layman, of its meaning or language. I am indebted to
my father's knowledge of Hebrew for its translation: "Sit thou on my
right hand!"

though only by way of short quotations. One of these was made apparently to tease Käthe, who goodhumoredly responded: "Good Heavens! Who said that?" The striking similarity of the Greek and German speech was pointed out by the reformer, who proved it by such examples as the cognate words ὑπέρ, μετά and σύν, and *über, mitt* and *sampt*, and the augment as seen in γέγραφα and *geschrieben*.[1]

Luther's colloquial German is very racy, with marked dialectical and conversational peculiarities. He evidently took no such care in his oral as he did in his written language to adopt the purest idiom. All this, as well as the frequent anacoluthon and solecism found in the original notes is smoothed off and standardized, so to speak, in the collection of Aurifaber.[2]

It is perhaps partly because of the lack of literary form in the Table Talk that we get such a perfect picture of Luther in it. Here we see him in all the simplicity and naïveté of his large-hearted German nature. "God has commanded us" he says, "that we should be simple, open, and true."[3] When Käthe was ill God made her well again, he who always gives what is best for his children and more than they can ask.[4] How fresh is this picture:

On the Sunday after St. Michael's day he was happy in mind, and joked with his friends and with me (Mathesius), and disparaged his own learning: "I am a fool," said he, "and you are cunning and wiser than I in economy and politics. For I do not apply myself to such things, but only to the Church and to getting the best of the Devil. I believe, however, if I did give myself to other sorts of business I could master them. But as I attend only to what is plain to view,

---

[1] Seidemann, *op. cit.*, p. 30.   [2] See Opitz, *Luthers Sprache*.

[3] Kroker, *op. cit.*, no. 48.

[4] *Ibid.*, no. 28. See also Preger, *op. cit.*, no. 6.

any one can get the better of me, until, indeed, I see he is a thief, and then he can't cheat me." [1]

Luther is as frank as he is simple; there is nothing in his own life, no opinion of men or books,[2] no recess of religious feeling which he is not willing to talk about. His Table Talk outdoes Rousseau in frankness, though it must always be remembered that Luther would never have thought of publishing the details of his life which Rousseau made the materials of his confessions. One passage, which also casts an interesting sidelight on Luther's marriage, is too good not to be quoted.

He spoke as follows [*in 1538*] *of his own marriage:* Had I wished to marry fourteen years ago I should have chosen the wife of Basilius, Anna of Schonfeld. I never loved my own wife, but suspected her of being proud, as she is; but God willed that I should show mercy to the poor fugitive, and by his grace it turned out that my marriage was most happy.[3]

This must not be taken to indicate that Luther did not love

---

[1] "Sontag post Michaelis ex animo laetus erat et jocabatur cum amicis et mecum et extenuebat suam eruditionem: ' Ich bin alber, saget er, und ir seit ein schalck und gelerter als ich in rebus oeconomicis et politicis. Denn ich nim mich der sachen nicht an und hab mit der ecclesia zu schaffen, und muss dem Teuffel auf die schantze sehen. [See Grimm, *Deutsches Wörterbuch*, vol. viii, p. 2164.] Das glaub ich, wenn ich mich auf die andern hendeln gebe, ich wolts auch mercken. Ich glaub eim itzlichen, drumb kan man mich wol bescheissen; alsbaldt ich mich aber fur einem fürsehe, der nimpt mir nichts.'" Kroker, *op. cit.*, no. 430.

[2] His free criticism of the Bible is well known. See *e. g.*, a liberal opinion of Ezekiel in Preger, *op. cit.*, no. 37.

[3] Khumer, p. 381, quoted by Seidemann, *op. cit.*, p. 162, note. A confused account of the same is given in Bindseil, *op. cit.*, ii, 338. Köstlin (*op. cit.*, vol. i, p. 762) quotes from Bindseil, and hence gets the wrong account, giving the name *"Ave"* instead of *"Anna."*

his wife after their marriage; the Table Talk is full of instances of exemplary conjugal devotion and he told Dietrich he would not change Käthe for France and Venice.[1]

Sometimes this simplicity shows itself in a sort of naïveté and lack of the critical point of view.

I would give the world [he says] to have the stories of the antediluvian patriarchs also, so that we could see how they lived, preached, and suffered. . . . I have taught and suffered too, but only fifteen, or twenty, or thirty years; they lived seven or eight hundred or more, and how they must have suffered![2]

His way of regarding the French mode of address is hardly more sophisticated.

The question was mooted whether it was a sin to curse a Frenchman. For they themselves have the custom of greeting their dearest friends with a curse, as " Pest and pox take you, sir!" Was it, then, a sin when the mind was free from hatred? He replied: " Our speech should be Yea and Nay, and the name of the Lord is not to be taken in vain. But it may be that their curses are more innocent than many a good-morning with us."[3]

In oral discourse the Reformer showed a marked predilection for the sententious style. Apophthegm and anecdote abound in the Colloquies. Many of those good stories current with us, whose origin is lost in the dimness of antiquity, appear in some form or other. The anecdote of the emperor who considered himself superior by his official position to the rules of grammar, last used to attack President

---

[1] Dietrich, Dec. 3, 1534. Quoted Köstlin, *op. cit.*, vol. ii, p. 497.

[2] Bindseil, *op. cit.*, vol. i, p. 82.

[3] Seidemann, *op. cit.*, p. 85.

Roosevelt's spelling reform, is related by Luther and attributed to Sigismund.[1] Another story, current before his time, and taken from him by Browning is that of the two brothers *Date* and *Dabitur vobis.*[2]

One of the pleasantest qualities of the Table Talk is the humor which is constantly appearing. Unfortunately most of the witticisms have been eliminated from the later collections, with their serious purpose of edification, and can only be read in the sources. Luther was naturally of a joyous disposition, "*ein hurtiger und fröhlicher junger Gesell,*" as Mathesius calls him.[3] Much of the exuberance of his high spirits, which had been crushed out in his youth by physical and mental suffering appeared fully in his later life.

Joy and good humor with reverence and moderation is the best medicine for a young man—yea, for all men. I, who have passed my life with mourning and a sad face, now seek and accept joy wherever I can find it.[4]

His jokes were never "practical" or rough, but they were often personal, as when he compares Pommer's preaching to an underdone meal.[5] He loved to poke good-humored fun at Käthe, who took it well and showed by her quick wit in repartee she did not get the worst of it.[6] Her loquacity, real or imagined, was the subject of occasional

---

[1] Bindseil, *op. cit.*, vol. i, p. 154.

[2] Kroker, *op. cit.*, no. 452. Browning: "The Twins."

[3] E. Rolffs: "Luther's Humor ein Stuck seiner Religion," in *Preus. Jahrb.*, 1904, vol. 115, pp. 468-488. See p. 468 for this. The author writes charmingly but misses the great source of Luther's humor in quoting from his letters only. He finds Luther's humor "idyllic."

[4] *Ibid.*, p. 487.

[5] Kroker, *op. cit.*, no. 99.

[6] See *supra*, p. 72, and Kroker, *op. cit.*, no. 332.

jest; one day Luther recommended her to an Englishman who wanted to learn German as his tutor because " she is so copiously eloquent that she beats me all to pieces." [1] Luther humorously recognizes that she is head of the household, comparing her to Moses and himself to Aaron. [2]

Jokes on religious subjects go rather further than those of a thoroughly correct reformer should. In one passage Luther facetiously compares three famous preachers of his day to the Trinity: " They are one essence and three persons, Pomer the Father, Crodel the Son, and Rörer the Holy Ghost." [3]

This of course is with us a matter of taste, and it is just in matters of taste that Luther shows himself the child not only of his age but of his class.   Luther spoke out whether in describing the morals of the Italians,[4] or his own ailments [5] or in giving advice to one tempted.[6]   He spoke out too, in giving his opinions of his enemies and those of the Gospel in language which has never been surpassed and rarely equalled for invective force.[7]   These defects have been so elaborately apologized for by editor and translator that they have perhaps attained undue prominence.   Whatever he was Luther was not vicious, and we never see that *polisonnerie* which is so plain in Erasmus, for example. We do not find Luther writing enthusiastically to a friend

[1] Seidemann, *op. cit.*, p. 156.

[2] Kroker, *op. cit.*, no. 53.   An example of the same kind given by Rolffs from a letter addressed to " Meiner herzlieben Hausfrauen Katherin Lutherin Doctorin Zulsdorferin Säumärkterin und was sie mehr sein kann." Rolffs, *loc. cit.*, p. 483.

[3] Kroker, *op. cit.*, no. 94.

[4] Seidemann, *op. cit.*, p. 53.

[5] With a satire on the physician.   Seidemann, *op. cit.*, p. 139.

[6] Kroker, *op. cit.*, no. 737e.

[7] See J. H. Robinson: " The Study of the Lutheran Revolt," in *American Hist. Rev.*, Jan., 1903.

about the kisses he has enjoyed [1] or wittily toying with the vicious propensities of mankind in the style of the *Praise of Folly*. Luther was considered remarkably pure in his own age. Mathesius relates that he never heard from him one shameful word,[2] a judgment in which any fair-minded reader will concur; Luther was frank, but he was not prurient.

As to invective, Luther only gave as good as he got. He speaks sometimes of the revolting slanders circulated against him.[3] Sometimes he showed an admirable, as well as a wise, self-restraint in this respect, as when, after reading the scurrilous attack of Cochlaeus he decided not to answer it. " I shall not answer Cochlaeus' book against me, and he will then be much angrier than if I did, for he will not get the honor he thought." [4]

[1] F. M. Nichols, *Epistles of Erasmus*, p. 203. To us, perhaps, Erasmus seems the less excusable; to the eighteenth century Luther would have been the more unpleasing. *Cf.* Voltaire's *Lettres à son Altesse le Prince de . . . . . sur Rabelais*. His strictures are certainly satirical, but we get a true note when he says " Swift is the Rabelais of gentlemen," thereby implying that the indecency of the latter (who resembled, though he far outdid, Luther in this respect) was not quite polished enough for good society.

[2] Mathesius, *Luther Histories*, 1570, p. 136a, quoted by Lösche, *Analecta*, p. 2.

[3] Wrampelmeyer, *op. cit.*, no. 1738, etc.

[4] Bindseil, *op. cit.*, vol. i, p. 147. The book was: *Sieben kopffe Martin Luthers von acht hohen sachen des Christlichen glaubens durch Doct. Jo. Cochleum*, 1529. In another place (Bindseil, *op. cit.*, vol. i, p. 438 *et seq.*) we have an account which seems more doubtful. It makes Luther contradict himself in consecutive sentences, due to the fact that Lauterbach here, as often, blended two accounts of the same thing. " I shall mortify Cochlaeus by silence and conquer him by contempt, for he is a mere fool, worth nothing in either scripture or dialectic; it would be a shame if I should answer his loose lies. . . . The book stinks; I am waiting to answer it until I can get time to answer the whole at once, so that I can do it with new, fresh wrath. He bores me as with a gimlet, but he will make a bunghole [*sc.* out of which my wrath shall flow]."

It is hardly fair to judge a man by his confidential and casual utterances. What Luther meant only for his friends' ears was bruited over Christendom as loudly as his deliberate opinions, meant for the world. He was a man of frank, open nature, much subject to the impression of the moment, often self-contradictory, careless of his own reputation. He never paused to weigh his conversation in a company as sympathetic and indulgent as he was confidential.[1] It is not fair to say, with a French writer,[2] that Luther talked along after dinner " *dans une demi-ivresse* " but we can readily understand that the influences of digestion and malt liquor were not always conducive to an austere observance of the proprieties. On the whole, if we judge him by his words, making allowance, as we must, for the age he lived in, and the circumstances of his education, Luther offers very little indeed whereby he can be condemned.[3]

---

[1] " No wonder some impertinent things might intermix themselves *liberius dicta* to refresh and recreate the company." *Supra*, p. 79.

[2] Brunet, *Propos de Table, Int.* On his drinking, see Köstlin, *op. cit.*, vol. ii, p. 506. It appears that he took too much *once*.

[3] *Cf.* Michelet quoted by Brunet, *op. cit.*, Introduction. Also Walch, *op. cit.*, vol. xxii, Einl., p. 33, quoting Selneccer's sententious remark " that we should not let a few weeds spoil the whole garden for us."

CHAPTER IX

THE TABLE TALK IN HISTORY

THE various sources and collections of *Tischreden* are not only literary monuments but historical documents, and in this chapter we shall treat them as such, showing first what use has been made of them by historians, then discussing their authenticity and reliability, and finally pointing out by a few specimens the kind of value they possess for the student of the Protestant Revolt.

Luther's enemies have always found in the Table Talk a trenchant weapon for attacking his character and doctrines. Even in his writings Luther is neither consistent nor temperate, much more in his private conversation is he careless and unguarded. By taking every thoughtless remark to a friend literally and with no attention to the context, the occasion on which it was uttered, and the cause which evoked it, it is easy enough to entangle Luther in a hopeless mass of contradictions and to asperse his character. This was done by Catholics and humanists as soon as the *Tischreden* were published, and subsequently has been undertaken more thoroughly by more scientific though equally hostile historians.[1]

Döllinger gives us a beautiful anthology of all the least considered and most infelicitous of Luther's sayings,

---

[1] "The gnat-like tribe of Janssenists," as Lösche (*Analecta*, Einl. *init.*) calls them, not without animus. For the humanist attack, see Walch, *op. cit.*, vol. xxii, p. 20.

whether taken from his works or from the Table Talk.
If, in a moment of despondency, Luther says the preaching
of the Gospel only seems to make men worse, and that the
converts to the new church abuse their liberty and commit
all manner of sin, *that* is taken as a serious effort to sum up
the effect of the reformed teaching and as a damning indict-
ment against it.[1] " It is a wonderful thing," says Luther
again, " and a sad one (*plena offendiculo*) that as the Gospel flourishes the world becomes ever worse, for all turn
spiritual liberty into license. For the reign of Satan and
the Pope suits this world . . . in truth, it degenerates under the doctrine of grace." [2] This of course is a full proof,
to the enemies of Protestantism, that the Revolt had a bad
moral effect. The same is shown still more clearly in Luther's impatient denunciation of the Protestant clergy as
full of " *faule, schädliche, schändliche, fleischliche Frei-
heit.*" [3]

Döllinger is content with quoting Luther's sayings
against himself, without putting a strained construction on
them. The recently published book of Father Denifle puts
an unnatural meaning on much that he said and thus attacks
Luther's life and character with such perverse erudition and
such an obvious lack of impartiality that it appears more
like the pamphlet of a violent contemporary than a serious
history. One example will suffice: *crimine ab uno disce
omnes.* The Reformer's words " *misceor feminis* " which
from the context obviously mean nothing else than that the
reformer no more lives in monastic retirement, but mixes

[1] Döllinger, *Die Reformation, ihre innere Entwickelung*, 1853-4, vol.
i, p. 295. Quoting Walch, *op. cit.*, vol. xvi, p. 2013.

[2] *Ibid.*, p. 320, quoting Bindseil, *op. cit.*, vol. i, p. 172.

[3] *Ibid.*, p. 306, quoting from the *Tischreden*.

with society, including that of women, are taken as a confession of habitual immorality.[1]

Protestant historians have used the Table Talk in a fairer and more amiable way, though it is true that they have occasionally been led by admiration of their hero to explain away what might damage his character. This has been done mainly by the editors; the historians proper have simply ignored the less admirable part of the Table Talk, or excused it all in a few general terms, while reserving their specific quotations for those sayings which show the brighter side of Luther's character. The editors, however, had to treat each saying by itself, and many of them have taken liberties with the text in the interests of piety. The first editor, Aurifaber, suppressed much he thought unedifying, as we can see by comparing him with his sources, and the last editor, Kroker, has shown the same tendency in supporting a reading in Mathesius's Luther Histories, recorded so many years later, against one taken on the spot, all in the interest of Luther's reputation.[2]

Of all the historians whom I have consulted [3] Köstlin has made the best use of the Table Talk. He used all the sources known at the time he wrote (*i. e.* all but the Mathesian collection, recently edited by Kroker) and he used them almost exhaustively. It is literally true that nearly every page of his biography has some reference to the Table Talk, and after comparing a large number of his

---

[1] H. P. Denifle, *Luther und Lutherthum*, 2 vols., 1904, 1905. This expression, taken from one of Luther's letters, is found on page 283 of vol. i. Many references are taken from the *Tischreden*.

[2] In the passage about Luther's "tres malos canes," quoted *supra*, p. 49, note 3.

[3] *E. g.*, Hausrath, *Luthers Leben* (last ed., 1905). Berger, *Martin Luther in kulturgeschichtliche Darstellung*, 1895. Kolde, *Martin Luther*, 1884, 1893. Lindsay, *Luther and the German Reformation*, 1900.

references with the originals, I can only testify my admiration for his thoroughness and fairness.[1]

The unprincipled use of the *Tischreden* by Luther's enemies led to an early attempt on the part of those of his friends whose zeal outran their judgment, to deny their genuineness and to impute them to Catholic forgers.[2] The attempt was so utterly preposterous that it was soon abandoned, and indeed is hardly worth mentioning. The authenticity of the Table Talk (making allowance for very slight editorial changes) is as indisputable as that of the *Address to the Christian Nobility*.

Another set of defenders admitting the authenticity of the work, have expressed their regret that it should ever have been published, and even suggested that the extant editions be suppressed—a proposal as impractical as injudicious.[3] If their real defence, which, as has been stated, lies in a comprehension of the conditions under which they were spoken, be once understood and fairly applied, no partisan friend of Luther (needless to say no impartial historian) will regret their publication.

A very different question from the genuineness of the Table Talk is the question of its reliability. In using this source the historian should give to statements of fact only such weight as can be given to any oral testimony. When the difference between the date of the fact recounted, and the

---

[1] See Köstlin, *op. cit.*, vol. i, p. 774, and vol. ii, p. 487 *et seq.*

[2] This was the object of a little work by Möller and Strickner, *De auctoritate libri scripti sub titulo Colloquiorum Mensalium Lutheri*, 1693. Walch (*op. cit.*, vol. xxii, Einl., p. 22 *et seq.*) quotes opinions of the same kind, summing up strongly in favor of the genuineness. Since his work, 1743, no editor has thought it necessary to take up the question.

[3] *Ibid.*, p. 25. Walch defends his own edition by saying it is better to have a good than a bad one.

date of the saying in which it is recorded can be ascertained, the probable degree of accuracy can be calculated. Obviously Luther's story of the Diet of Worms, told by him twenty years after it happened, is worth less than the account of his controversy with the Swiss, taken down within a few weeks of its occurrence.

The date can only be told as a rule, in the sources, and so it is these sources only, and not the collections, that must be used by the historian. Another reason for using them is that they contain the best text of the Table Talk. Again it is plain that the facts are reliable in proportion as they came within the personal observation of Luther and his guests. The not infrequent accounts of the evolutions of the Turkish army, and of the counter moves of Ferdinand and the German Princes, are worth no more than pure fiction as regards the facts they purport to record. They are worth something, however, as indicating the popular anxiety caused by the Turks in Germany in the sixteenth century, and the popular opinion that Ferdinand used these terrors to wring armies and supplies from the German States.[1]

This observation leads us to remark that it is not as a repertory of dates and figures, or as a chronicle of important historical events, that the Table Talk has its value. This lies rather in the brilliant picture it gives of the opinions, the motives, the reading, the daily life and personal attitude of the greatest German of his age, and in their portrayal of contemporary social life and habit.[2]

A good example of the value of the *Tischreden* is seen in the new light cast, by the recently published Mathesian

[1] *Cf.* Kroker, *op. cit.*, no. 507. Seidemann, *op. cit.*, 3 and 126.

[2] Making due allowance for the context and spirit of the documents.

Collection, on the vexed question of Luther's attitude to Philip of Hesse's bigamy. Here we get a few new facts, as for example that the Landgrave visited Weimar to discuss the project with Luther and Melanchthon, for which the *Tischreden* are the only authority.[1] The visit must have taken place in April, 1534, and the conversation reported by Mathesius who relates it, took place about June 1, 1540, so that it is quite possible that there may be a mistake in Luther's memory. More valuable, however, than a few doubtful facts of this nature, is the light cast on Luther's whole attitude by his continual reference to the unfortunate affair. We can see how perplexed he is about it, and what pressure must have been brought to bear to get him to accede to the second marriage. We regret to note, at the same time, that he seems more worried by the use the " Papists " make of the affair than by its doubtful morality. Fouchet's " worse than a crime, a blunder " is paralleled by his " not only a sin but a scandal."[2] His chief defence of his attitude is by comparison with the worse morality of the Papists. He is firmly convinced that all would have been well if the matter could have been kept quiet as he advised.[3]

Luther's characterization of his contemporaries is always interesting to us, not as a final valuation, but as evidence of Luther's relations with them. His opinion of the rela-

---

[1] Kroker, *op. cit.*, no. 181, note 11.

[2] " *Si Macedo peccavit, peccatum est et scandalum,*" Kroker, *op. cit.*, no. 241.

[3] See Kroker, *op. cit.*, nos. 181, 188, 233, 241, 245, *etc.* The most recent monograph on the subject, W. W. Rockwell's *Die Doppelehe des Landgrafen Philipp v. Hessen*, 1904, quotes Kroker's *Tischreden* in this connection as a source. He corrects many former misconceptions and shows that at the Eisenach meeting (July, 1540, shortly after the saying above quoted had been recorded) Luther advised " a good strong lie."

tive merits of himself and three other leaders is seen in his
calling Melanchthon "Deeds and words," Erasmus "Words
without deeds," himself " Deeds without words " and Carl-
stadt " Neither deeds nor words." [1]   Erasmus always ex-
cites his wrath, being (if we may borrow a phrase from
Milton) one of those lukewarm persons " who give God
himself the vomit."

I condoned all his boasts, [says Luther in one place,] but I could
not stand his catechism, because he teaches nothing certain in
it, but tries to make the youthful reader doubtful.   It was the
Roman curia and Epicurus who showed him the way.   In
Germany we have a regular fraternity of Epicureans, Crotus,
Mutianus and Justus Menius.[2]

Less than anything else Luther was able to understand or
sympathize with the advocate of half-way measures.   Of
Bucer he has a poor opinion;

That little wretch (*Leckerlein*) has no credit with me.   I
don't trust him, for he has too often betrayed me.   He showed
himself up badly at Regensburg, when he wanted to be a medi-
ator between me and the Pope, and said: " It is too bad that
there should be so much trouble for the sake of two or three
little articles!" [3]

Hardly less interesting than his opinion of his contemporaries is his opinion of men of former generations.   As
is well known his estimation of Aristotle was small, a natural reaction against the schoolmen.

---

[1] For this and a number of other characterizations, see Bindseil, *op.
cit.*, vol. i, pp. 266-306.

[2] Seidemann, *op. cit.*, p. 48.   For another of the same tenor, see
Kroker, *op. cit.*, no. 569.

[3] Kroker, *op. cit.*, no. 543.   For Agricola, see Seidemann, *op. cit.*, p.
70.   For Oecolampadius, Kroker, *op. cit.*, no. 468.

Aristotle is nothing but Epicurus. He does not believe that God cares for the world, or if he does, he thinks that God drowses along like a sleepy maid rocking a baby. Cicero was much better; in my opinion he got all that was best in the Greeks.[1]

Terence was his favorite author among the heathen and in the following opinion of him we see a venerable sanction for the joke on the mother-in-law, which still makes so large a part of current humor:

The *Hecyra* is a fine comedy, the best in Terence, but because it has no action it does not please the common student. But it is full of grave sententious sayings, useful for common life, such as: "All mothers-in-law hate their daughters-in-law." [2]

The Translation of the Bible naturally occupies much of his thought. In one place he lays down a sensible rule of translation which partly explains the success of his own:

It is not sufficient (in translation) to know the grammar and observe the sense of the words, but knowledge of the subject treated is essential to a proper understanding of the words. Lawyers do not understand the law except by practice, and no one can understand Virgil's Eclogues without knowing something of the subject. If the reader knows whether the eclogue is about Augustus or Cæsar, he can easily apply the words. So in the Bible I keep to the sense.[3]

[1] Kroker, *op. cit.*, no. 525.

[2] Kroker, *op. cit.*, no. 485. His allusions to Terence are quite frequent. In one place (if my memory serves me) he said he read a little of that author every day.

[3] *Ibid.*, no. 145. Further examples of the pains the Bible cost him and his estimate of previous translations are found in *ibid.*, nos. 470, 473. See also Dietrich, p. 137, quoted by Köstlin, *op. cit.*, vol. i, p. 86, note 2, for his opinion of the commentators on the Bible.

Some will contend that he carried this principle too far when he inserted a word in Romans which Paul had not used.

He often speaks of the part he took in the great historic events of Worms and Augsburg, and though his memory may be at fault as to details, his allusions are always worth much as illustrations of his later attitude. At one time he was inclined to make the Diet of Augsburg of 1518 the turning-point of his life. " Up to that time I knew too little of the errors of the Papacy." Possibly he exaggerated the amount of pressure brought to bear on him to retract.[1]

In like manner his memory of Worms is doubtless somewhat at fault, but his account of it is interesting as showing his later, more advanced attitude. As he remembered it he said:

Most gracious Lord Emperor: Some of my books are disputations (*Zanckbücher*), some didactic. The didactic and the word of God I will not recant, but if I have been too vehement against any one in disputation, or have said too much, I will let it be shown me if you give me time for reflection.

This, of course, contradicts the usual statement that he apologized for the invective and asked for time on the other.[2]

For the daily course of his private life the Table Talk is the best source we have. Even Luther's letters, frank,

---

[1] Seidemann, pp. 93-97. The Diet of 1518 is of course meant. He states that he was there three days without a safe-conduct. He arrived just at the close of the session. *Cambridge Modern History*, vol. ii, p. 133.

[2] Bindseil, *op. cit.*, vol. i, pp. 438-440. The passage cannot be dated with certainty. Of the same kind of reminiscence as the above is his account of his vow to be a monk. *Ibid.*, vol. iii, p. 187 *et seq.*

charming, intimate as they are, do not give us such a picture of him as does this record of his conversations. For some years such as 1538, we can tell just what he was thinking and doing on almost every day. Out of a wealth of material sufficient to construct a biography, we shall select a few specimens.

Luther's ill-health is a well-known fact, but we do not realize how constant and wearing it was until we read the Table Talk, where it is often alluded to, though never in anything but a brave and manly way. He suffered hardly less from his ailments than from the barbarous remedies of the time. Vertigo troubled him, for which he found help in a little food, remarking that butter was a good thing.[1] A more serious complaint was the ulceration of his body; he once compared his sores to the stars in the sky, saying that there were over two hundred of them.[2] At another time he wished he had died at Schmalkald, where he was tortured by the stone. His observation that medicine was a good thing but the doctors poor, was fully justified by the treatment he received on this occasion.[3]

His superstition, too, is constantly appearing. He had the tendency (common to the unscientific mind) of attributing what he could not explain to supernatural causes. Even a thunderstorm transcends natural phenomena. He said of one: " It is simply satanic. I believe the devils wanted to have a dispute and that some angel interposed this χάσμα and so tore their propositions up." Sometimes his credulity takes an active form which shocks our modern

---

[1] Bindseil, *op. cit.*, vol. i, p. 95.

[2] *Ibid.*, vol. i, p. 308.

[3] Seidemann, *op. cit.*, p. 24. See also Kroker, *op. cit.*, no. 747. For his illness in Italy, see Seidemann, *op. cit.*, p. 105. His best cure, he said, was John iii. 16. Dietrich, p. 119, quoted Köstlin, *op. cit.*, vol. ii, p. 505.

humanity. He advised, for example, that a poor girl who was said to shed tears of blood in the presence of another woman be tortured as a witch.[1] His advice as to how to frustrate the machinations of the spirits who stole the milk is more disgusting, though less cruel.[2] Sometimes he took a rational view as when he said the stars did not influence events.[3]

Luther's hospitality is strikingly portrayed in the Table Talk. In fact he must have had many guests all the time, or else he could not have had so many records made of his conversation by different persons. Not only did he have his friends with him for long periods together, but many chance visitors put up at his house. Such was the Swiss Superintendent whom Luther received on April 15, 1538. We have an agreeable evidence of his courtesy on this occasion in the delicacy with which he speaks of his relations with the Swiss Reformers.[4]

We have already spoken of his carelessness in temporal affairs and the anxiety it caused his good wife, but the frequency of its reappearance in the Table Talk will perhaps justify us in adducing another example. Käthe complained that she had only three bottles of beer left, to which he complacently replied:

God can easily make them four. If he were not our provider, we should soon be done for. I have an extraordinary way of living, spending more than I get. For I must spend more than 500 florins[5] a year in the kitchen, without counting

---

[1] Seidemann, *op. cit.*, p. 117. "Let such be tortured"; perhaps he means the other woman, or both.

[2] *Ibid.*, p. 121. [3] *Ibid.*, p. 47.

[4] *Ibid.*, p. 62. See also Kolde, *Analecta Lutherana*, p. 378, on the *miscellanea turba* of old and young in Luther's house.

[5] *I. e.*, the amount of his income, 200 florins besides the 300 he got from the elector.

clothes and extras. If I had a smaller house I would keep away the multitude and be as private as I could. But God is the provider for simple folk." [1]

On his relations with his wife and children much may be gathered from the Table Talk, but the subject is already hackneyed. He may joke his wife about her womanly readiness in speech,[2] or pun on her name, calling her his *Cathena*, or Chain, but we feel that it is all good-humored and affectionate. As we have seen Käthe was not always on the best terms with the students, and they undoubtedly retaliated for her jealousy by the depreciatory tone in which they refer to her.[3]

It is interesting to observe how much our appreciation of the comparative worth of the different sayings has changed from that of Luther's contemporaries. To the first editors those sayings were most valuable which gave an authoritative exposition of some knotty point in theology, or an exegesis of some obscure text in the Bible. To us these once vital questions have sunk into comparative neglect, and what Luther may have thought of the Judgment Day,[4] or of Nebuchadnezzar [5] is no longer decisive, hardly interesting. To all who know Luther, however (and who does not?), those stories and jokes, the familiar conversations which reveal so much of the man's heart and life, will have an ever fresh and abiding interest.

[1] Bindseil, *op. cit.*, vol. iii, p. 199.

[2] Wrampelmeyer, *op. cit.*, no. 111 *et seq.*

[3] See *supra*, ch. ii and iii. *Cf.* Wrampelmeyer, *op. cit.*, no. 120. Köstlin, *op. cit.*, vol. ii, p. 496.

[4] Kroker, *op. cit.*, no. 122.

[5] *Ibid.*, no. 218.

APPENDIX

BIBLIOGRAPHY

THIS bibliography is divided into six parts. The first is a catalogue of the MSS. and editions of the sources. The second is a similar catalogue of the collections, in the various MSS. and editions. The third part gives a table showing the relations of the various MSS., how the notebooks were gradually combined into the later collections. Part four is a list of all the German and Latin printed editions, both collections and sources. The fifth part is a catalogue of the English and French translations. The sixth and last section is a review of additional explanatory material bearing on the subject. My account of this last category is critical as well as descriptive; the other classes of material have been so fully treated in the text as to render further criticism unnecessary.[1]

PART I. THE SOURCES
Cordatus

1. *Tagebuch über Martin Luther*, geführet von Conrad Cordatus. MS. found by Dr. H. Wrampelmeyer in the Church Library at Zellerfeld. It contains a variety of material besides *Tischreden*. At one time Wrampelmeyer be-

---

[1] I have seen none of the MSS. myself; my account is, therefore, taken from the printed sources indicated in the notes.

lieved it to have been in the handwriting of Cordatus, but later found that it was not.[1]

2. *Die Herliche Schöne und Liebliche Apophtegmata des Hochgelaerhtens Docto. Martini. Lutheri,* zusammen geschrieben Per Dominum Doctorem Conradum Cordatum. " Haec varia et utillissima dicta sanctissimi viri Doctoris Martini Lutheri scribebat sibi Sebastian. Redlich Bernoënsis, M. D., LXVI."[2]

Dietrich

3. *Collecta ex Colloquiis habitis cum D. Martino Luthero in mensa per annos sex, quibus cum eo Wittenberge communitus sum usus.* 29, 30, 31, 32, 34, 35. MS. Cent. V. append. no. 75, Nürnberg.[3] The numbers 29, 30, etc., refer to the years 1529, etc.

4. *Rapsodiae et dicta quaedam ex ore Doctoris Martini Lutheri in familiaribus colloquiis annotata* . . . Valentinus Bavarus suo labore et manu propria in hunc librum transcribendo comparavit. 1548. MS. in the Royal Library of Gotha.[4]

5. *Colloquia Lutheri conscripta a quibusdam et alia quaedam addita sunt. Thesaurus Theologiae* 1543. Christopherus Obenander, Studio Witten. 44.[5] MS. in Royal Library at Dresden.

Schlaginhaufen

6. *Martini Lutheri Privata Dicta, Consilia, Judicia,*

---

[1] Wrampelmeyer, *op. cit.*, pp. 6-12.

[2] MS. first noticed by Kawerau. *Cf.* Wrampelmeyer, *op. cit.*, Einl., p. 10, note 1; Kroker, *op. cit.*, Einl., p. 35 *et seq.;* Lösche, *Analecta*, p. 4, note 1. Redlich of Berne is otherwise unknown.

[3] Seidemann, *op. cit.*, Einl., p. xi. Preger, *op. cit.*, Einl., p. xviii.

[4] Kroker, *op. cit.*, Einl., p. xxi.

[5] *Ibid.*, Einl., p. xxii. Bindseil, *op. cit.*, p. cxxii.

Vaticinia, Item Epistolae, Sales, Consolationes hince inde collectae, Anno 1567. MS. Clm. 943 in the Munich Public Library.[1]

Lauterbach

7. *Tagebuch auf das Jahr 1538.* MS. in Royal Library at Dresden.[2]

8. *Meditationes et Colloquia D. Lutheri.* MS. in Stolbergische Bibliothek at Wernigerode.[3]

9. *Tagebuch*, copied by Khumer (Kummer), in Dresden Library, 1554.[4]

10. *Dicta et Facta R. D. D. Martini Lutheri et aliorum*, 1550. "Georgius Steinert hujus codicis est possessor." MS. in Munich, Clm. 937-939. Contains copies from Lauterbach, and others.[5]

11. *Colloquia Serotina D. M. L.*, 1536, 22 Octobris [and to 1539] descripta ex αὐτογράφῳ. D. Antonii Lauterbachii primi Superint. Pirn. in Misn. Anno 1553 manu Pauli Judicis al. Richteri primi Pastoris Neapol. s. Neostad. prope Pirnam. MS. at Gotha, B 169.[6]

Mathesius, Tagebuch

12. *Goth B. 168.* MS. in the Ducal Library at Gotha. Collection of Judgments of Luther on sundry things and persons, chiefly theological. P. 471. This MS. contains a great variety of things. It has many of Mathesius' notes.[7]

13. *Codex Rhedigeranus* of the City Library at Breslau

---

[1] Preger, *op. cit.*, Einl., pp. iv, v.

[2] Förstemann-Bindseil, *op. cit.*, vol. iv, p. xv *et seq.* Seidemann, *op. cit.*, Einl., p. iii.

[3] Seidemann, *op. cit.*, Einl., p. iii. Preger, *op. cit.*, Einl., p. i.

[4] *Ibid.*, p. ix.

[5] Preger, *op. cit.*, Einl., pp. xxii, xxiii.

[6] Kroker, *op. cit.*, p. xxii.

[7] Lösche, *op. cit.*, Einl., p. 24 *et seq.*

No. 295. It contains Mathesius' notes copied from X in almost exactly the same form as *Analecta.*[1]

14. *Familiaria Colloquia Rev. Viri D. D. Mar. Lutheri.* In possession of the book dealer Hirzel of Leipzig. This has quite a variety of things including many of Mathesius' notes " undoubtedly near the original " and a few of Lauterbach's.[1]

15. *Excerpta haec omnia in mensa ex ore D. Ma.: Luterj. Anno Domini* 1540. MS. in Nürnberg.[2]

Mathesius, Luther Histories

16. *Historien von des Ehrwirdigen in Gott seligen thewren Manns Gottes, Doctoris Martini Luthers, anfang, Lehr, leben unnd Sterben.* Nürnberg 1570. (Reprinted later, see *infra.*)

Plato

17. *Memorabilia dicta et facta Lutheri.* This MS. was used by Köstlin and cited by him as the *Leipz. Mskr.* Its age and author are unknown. The chirography is that of the later Reformation time. The latest datable piece (No. 214) speaks of the Diet of Augsburg, 1547.

It contains 218 Nos. Kroker proved these to come from Plato's collection. Among the *Tischreden* there are a number of anecdotes of the guests, Melanchthon, Bugenhagen, Major, Cruciger, Mathesius, &c. It is much the most original of the Plato copies. Kroker prints (*op. cit.*, 52, Einl.) four pieces from it which are found nowhere else.[3]

---

[1] Lösche, *op. cit.*, Einl., p. 24 *et seq.*

[2] Edited by Lösche, 1892, as *Analecta Lutherana et Melanthonia.* See *infra*, printed editions.

[3] Kroker, *op. cit.*, Einl., p. 1.

18. *Corpus Reformatorum*, vol. XX, pp. 519-608. Melanchthon's reports of Luther's sayings, described as "Certain histories recited by him in his public lectures, collected by a certain disciple, Weric Vendenhaimer of Nürnberg." These consist of 304 sayings taken mostly from Plato's collection.[1]

Miscellaneous

19. Zwickau N LXX. *Adiaphoristica item quadem apophthegmata.* MS. in Library of the Ratsschule.

20. Hamburg *Supellex epistolica Uffenbachii et Worliorum LXXIV. Ad historsam Reformationis spectantia.*

These two MSS. are of very minor importance, having only a few *Tischreden* in them.

PART II. THE COLLECTIONS

Mathesius

1. Eberhard. Freyberg in a school Programme of 1727 speaks of a MS. of Luther's Tischreden in his possession which is designated as "*Thesaurus Theologicus*," and came from the hand of C. Eberhard. This man was born 1523, at Schneeberg, and died 1575, at Wittenberg. He had copied it from the original of Mathesius, as he notes in an autograph inscription on a page glued to the cover: "Hunc librum descripsi ex. Dni. Magistri Mathesii libellis cui acceptum refero et gratias immortales ago. Caspar Eberhard 1550, Aprilis 27." This MS. is unfortunately lost. Dr. Schnorr, of Carolsfeld, advertised for it in vain, and so did Kroker.[2]

---

[1] Lösche, *Analecta*, Einl., p. 30 *et seq.* He mentions two other books in which he has found parallels to his own MS, but they are not properly sources at all.

[2] See Seidemann, *op. cit.*, p. ix, and Kroker, Einl., *op. cit.*, p. 38. Schnorr gave some references from Eberhard's life by D. T. Müller (1754) to show that he had written *Colloquia*.

2. *Luthers Tischreden in der Mathesischen Sammlung.*
This MS. was spoken of by Lingke, 1769. Lösche refers
to it as lost.[1] Kroker discovered it between two books in
the Leipzig Library, and edited it. Not mentioned in the
Catalogue of Leipzig MSS. by Naumann, 1838; it appears
in the catalogue of Pölitz's Library as follows: *Luth.
Martinus, Colloquia. Manuscripta Collecta*, 1546. In 1885
G. Wustmann printed a little bit of it, naming both Mathesius and Schiefer in connection with it, but this indication
of its whereabouts remained unnoticed.

Unknown

1. *Farrago litterarum ad amicos et colloquiorum in
mensa RP Domini Martini Lutheri &c. MS.* in ducal library
of Gotha. On the binding is, M. B. 1551. See *supra, p.* 57.

Lauterbach

1. Halle MS. written 1560, edited by Bindseil, 1863-66.
Contains the first redaction of Lauterbach's collection. See
above, chapter on collections, and below, printed editions.
Found in the library of the Orphan Asylum at Halle.
Folio 654 Bl. Very poor hand. The sections often run
together. Said to have been edited with " painful accuracy." [2]

2. Dresden A 91 & 92. Two volumes folio of 283 and
365 pages respectively. Anno 1562.

3. Gotha A 262. MS. at Gotha, an incomplete copy of
second part of the above. Folio 310 Bl.

4. *Colloquia Meditationes &c. Lutheri.* Edited by Reb-

---

[1] Lingke: *Luthers Merkwürdige Reisegeschichte*, Einl., p. 3. Seidemann, *op cit.*, Einl., p. xii, gives numerous references on Werndorf and
Schiefer. Lösche, *Analecta*, p. 10. Kroker, *op. cit.*, Einl., p. 17.

[2] Bindseil, *op. cit.*, Einl., *passim.* Meyer, *loc. cit.*, p. 6.

enstock at Frankfurt a. M. 1571. See chapter on collections and *infra*, printed editions.

5. MS. in Wolfenbüttel of 1562. Extra 72. Two parts of 169 and 236 pages respectively. It contains some matter besides *Tischreden*.[1]

Aurifaber

1. *Deutsche Tischreden*, printed 1566 *et saepe*. See chapter on collections and below, printed editions.

2. C germ. 4502 in Munich. Anno 1614. Two parts, 229 and 191 pages, octavo. Extracts from Aurifaber.[2]

3. Karlsruhe 437, *Luther's Tischreden* 1535-1542. Written *circa* 1575; contains extracts from the printed edition, with other matter in the appendices.[2]

PART III. THE RELATIONS OF THE MSS.

A Table showing the relations of the MSS. will be found opposite this page. The explanation of this table is as follows:

We start here with the twelve notetakers, and trace the process of transcription through which their notes went. We first observe that these transcriptions were not exact, the copyist changed both the matter and the order of what he copied, left out a good deal and introduced extraneous matter. We simply mean that the MSS. took most of their material from the sources indicated, though they often took much from others, especially, of course, in the large collections. A full description of the MSS. has already been given.

The *Tagebuch* of Cordatus is known in two MSS.

Dietrich kept a notebook, and also had a collection, copied from others. The former is known in the MS. *Dietrich*, the lost MS. *X* copied from both, and was the source of three other copies, *Bavarus*, *Obenander* and *Mathesius* § 6.

[1] Meyer, *loc. cit.*, p. 7.   Mentioned in Kroker, *op. cit.*, Einl., p. 37.
[2] Meyer, *loc. cit.*, p. 36.

Schlaginhaufen's *Tagebuch* was edited by Preger.
Lauterbach was the author of at least four sources. The
first *Tagebuch* was copied by Weller, both in his notebook and
his collection. The second was edited from a Dresden MS.
by Seidemann, and is also known in three other more or less
complete copies, *Khumer, Munich MS.*, and *Wernigerode MS.*
The third *Tagebuch* is known in the MS. *Serotina*, and also
in excerpts in the fifth section of Kroker. The fourth book
was a simple collection, *i. e.*, a book of copies from others,
which was taken into three of the MSS. which have the *Tagebuch of 1539, viz., Khumer, Munich,* and *Wernigerode*. From
one of these, or a MS. like them, Lauterbach made his large
collection, taking notes also from other sources doubtless,
especially from his own earlier notes, possibly through Weller.
The first redaction was edited from the *Halle MS.* by Bindseil.
The second is known in two copies, MSS. at *Gotha*, and *Dresden*. From another lost copy a third redaction was made and
edited by Rebenstock. By a fourth line a fourth redaction
was made, which we have in the *Wolfenbüttel MS.*, which was
the source of Aurifaber. Aurifaber also incorporated other
notes, especially important being his own and those of Stolz,
which are unknown in any other form.

Weller's *Tagebuch* and *Sammlung*, in both of which he
copied largely from Lauterbach, were incorporated into the
MS. published by Kroker, but in different ways.

Corvinus' notebook, if he had one, is lost. One of his notes
survives in Schlaginhaufen.

Mathesius was the author of two books of *Tischreden*, the
Tagebuch of 1540 and the *Luther Histories*. The first was
copied in a lost MS., *X*, and from it by four other extant MS.,
Gotha B., Hirzil, Rhedigeranus, and the one edited as *Analecta*
by Lösche. It was also copied by Plato, and incorporated by
Mathesius himself as the first section of his collection. The
other sources of this collection are indicated by lines; they
were all kept by Mathesius himself in a lost MS., *X*. This
was copied by Eberhard, whose MS. is lost, and also by Krüginger, who added to them his own copy of Weller, published
as § 8 of Mathesius in Kroker.

Heydenreich and Besold are known only in copies in the Mathesian Collection.

Plato was copied by Melanchthon, and taken from him as lecture notes by Vendenhaimer, whence they were reprinted in the *Corpus Reformatorum*. He was also copied by the MS. *Memorabilia*, and by Mathesius in the seventh section.

Stolz and Aurifaber, as has already been stated, survive only in the collection of the latter, where their notes cannot be distinguished from those taken from other sources.

Some MSS., such as *Hamburg, Zwickau*, and the collection *Farrago*, cannot be placed in this table at all, as their notes are either too few or their complexity too great to enable the investigator to determine their relations. They are all unimportant.

PART IV. PRINTED EDITIONS; GERMAN AND LATIN

Aurifaber

1. *Tischreden oder Colloquia Doct. Mart. Luthers*, so er in vielen Jaren, gegen gelarten Leuten, auch frembden Gesten, und seinen Tischgesellen gefüret, Nach den Heubtstucken unserer Chritlichen Lere, zusammen getragen. Eisleben. 1566.[1]

The *Tischreden* are divided here, as in all of Aurifaber's editions, into 80 great chapters. In this edition they are incorrectly numbered 82, nos. 23 and 32 being left out.

2. *The same*, Frankfurt am Mayn, 1567. Folio. Doubtless pirated.[1]

3. *The same*, Frankfurt am Mayn. Octave, 2 vols. Under the title we have: "Anfenglichs von Antonio Lauterbach zusammen getragen, Hernacher in gewisse Locos Communes verfasset und aus viel anderer Gelehrter Leuth Collectaneis gemehret Durch Herrn Joh. Aurifaber." This edition was also pirated.[1]

---

[1] Irmischer, *Luthers Tischreden, Sämt. Werke*, Frankfurt am Mayn und Erlangen, vol. 57, Einl., p. x *et seq.*

4. *The same,* Frankfurt am Mayn, 1568, folio. A new introduction, by Aurifaber, dated July 1, 1567, complains of changes and additions to his authentic volume of *Tischreden.* He probably alludes to the last two editions, though the changes in them are very slight.[1]

5. *The same,* Frankfurt am Mayn, 1569, folio. Appendix with prophecies of Luther collected by Mag. G. Walther, and subscription by J. Fink.[1]

6. *The same,* Eisleben, 1569. Folio.[2]

7. *The same,* Eisleben, 1577. Folio.[1]

8. *Tischreden von Martini Lutheri,* so er in vielen Jaren die Zeyt seines Lebens gegen Gelehrten Leuthen &c. Anfenglichs von M. Anthonio Lauterbach zusammen getragen. Hernacher in gewisse Locos Communes verfasset und aus viel anderer Gelehrter Leute Collectaneis gemehret durch Johannem Aurifabrum. Frankfurt am Mayn 1571.

This edition is not mentioned in Irmischer, Bindseil, or any other catalogue of the *Tischreden.* I have seen a copy at Union Seminary, New York, and there is another at Johns Hopkins University, Baltimore.

It is a pirated edition, copied mainly from no. 3, but with changes taken from no. 5. After Aurifaber's Preface of 1569 comes the register of 80 chapters, and at the end a sort of Appendix put in the Index as "Auch noch viel andere Tischreden Doct. Mart. Luth. zum theil in die obgesetzte Locos gehörende, von allerley Sachen, auss etlichen geschriebenen Büchern zusammen getragen."

At the end comes an Appendix of *Propheteyung* D. Martini Lutheri. Then the alphabetic Index. On the last page the colophon: *Gedruct zu Frankfurt am Mayn durch Peter Schmid und Sigismund Feyerabend.*

---

[1] Irmischer, *Luthers Tischreden, Sämt. Werke,* Frankfurt am Main und Erlangen, vol. 57, Einl., p. x *et seq.*

[2] *Ibid.* I have seen this edition at Union Theological Seminary.

Stangwald

9. *Tischreden doctor Mart. Luthers,* so er in vielen Jaren, gegen Gelärten Leuten, auch frembden Gesten, und seinen Tischgesellen geführet. Nach den Häupstücken unserer Christlichen Lehre, zusammen getragen. Und jetzt Auffs neuwe in ein richtige Ordnung gebracht, Und nach den geschriebenen Tischreden Doct. Mart. Luth. Corrigiert.

This title is followed by a picture of Luther at table with six men, four boys attending. Lower down on the page we see: *Gedruct zu Frankfurt am Mayn, durch Thomas Rebarts Seligen Erben* . . . (the sheet is torn at this point), and further down the date: *M. D. LXXI.*

Aurifaber's Preface then comes, dated July 7, 1569. The *Tischreden* themselves form a thick folio. They are divided into nine large sections, unnumbered, each section divided into several captions, numbered, making 43 captions in all, as against Aurifaber's 80; though about the same amount of material is in each.[1]

The name of the editor does not appear on the titlepage of this edition, but there is no doubt that it was Stangwald, as he speaks of it in his edition of 1591. In the preface to the latter edition he describes his work, and says he was led to undertake the redaction in order to get an edition closer to the original text.

10. *The same,* 1591, with name of editor on the titlepage, and preface explaining the method of improvement, from the notes of Mathesius and Mörlin. This edition was published at Jena.[2]

---

[1] I saw a copy of this edition at Harvard, where it was ascribed to Aurifaber in the catalogue until I pointed out to the librarian that it really belonged to Stangwald.

[2] Irmischer, *op. cit.,* xiii, xiv. Förstemann-Bindseil, *op. cit.,* vol. iv, p. xxviii.

11. *The same,* reprint at Leipzig by T. Steinmann, 1603.[1]

12. *The same,* 1621, at Leipzig, by B. Voigt. This has the colophon at the end, " Printed at Jena by T. Steinman, 1603." [2]

13. Edition of 1669 at Frankfurt a.M.[3]

14. *The same,* folio, 1700, at Leipzig.

15. *The same,* 1723, at Dresden and Leipzig. Georgisch in his *Bücher-Lexicon* gives the date as 1722.

Selneccer

16. *Colloquia, oder Christliche Nützliche Tischreden Doctoris Martini Lutheri,* so er in vielen Jaren, gegen Gelehrten Leuten, und frembden Gesten, und seinen Genossen, nach den Heuptstücken unserer Christlichen Lehre, gehalten. Erstlich durch M. Johannem Aurifabrum seligen, fleissig zusammengetragen und in Druck gegben: Jetzt auffs newe in ein richtige Ordnung gebracht, und also verfertiget, das sie allen Christen sehr nötig, nützlich, und tröstlich, sonderlich zu diesen elenden letzten zeiten, zu lesen sind. Sampt einer newen Vorrede, und kurtzen Beschreibung des Lebens und wandels Herrn Doctoris Lutheri, auch sehr nützlichem Register am Ende dieses Buchs angehenget, aller Bücher und Capitel der Göttlichen, heiligen schrifft, wo, und wenn dieselbigen der Herr Doctor Lutherus ausgelegt, und erkleret habe, und in welchen Tomis solche auslegung zu finden sei.

After a Latin couplet and the usual quotation from John 6 we see: Nic. Selneccerus. Leipsig, MDLXXVII.

---

[1] This is in the *British Museum Catalogue.* It is not spoken of in Irmischer, but its existence might be inferred from his description of no. 12, in which the colophon of this edition was taken over unchanged.

[2] Irmischer, *ibid.*

[3] This is known only through a note in Georgisch in his *Bücher-Lexicon,* quoted by Irmischer, *op. cit.,* p. xv.

After this Aurifaber's Preface of 1569 is inserted. Then an "*Historica Oratio*" on Luther's life.[1]

17. *The same*, 1580[1]
18. *The same*, 1581.[1]

Other German Editors

19. *D. Martin Luthers sowol in Deutscher als Lateinischer Sprache verfertigte und aus der letzteren in die erstere übersetzte Sämtliche Schriften.* Zwei und zwansigster Theil, Welcher die *Colloquia oder Tischreden*, so von Johann Aurifaber mit Fleiss zusammen getragen, und nach den Hauptstücken der Christlichen Lehre und Glaubens verfasset worden, enthält; Herausgegeben von Johann Georg Walch, der heiligen Schrift D. und Prof. Publ. Ordin. auf der Universität Jena, wie auch Hochfürstl. Sächs. und Brandenb. Onolzb. Kirchen- und Consistorial-Rath. Halle im Magdeburgischen. Druckts und verlegts Joh. Justinus Gebauer. 1743.

This was the 22d volume of his edition of the *Sämtliche Werke*, which began to come out 1740.[2]

20. *Dr. Martin Luthers Sinnreiche Tischreden.* Nach den Hauptstücken christlicher Lehre verfasst. Neue, wohlfeile Ausgabe. 2 Bde. Stuttgart und Leipzig. Verlag von L. F. Nieger und Comp. 1836.[3]

21. *D. Martin Luthers Tischreden oder Colloquia,* so er in vielen Jahren gegen gelahrten Leuten, auch frembden Gästen und seinen Tischgesellen geführet, nach den Hauptstücken unserer Christlichen Lehre zusammen getragen.

---

[1] Irmischer, *op. cit.*, vol. 57, p. xv.
[2] These editions are common.
[3] Irmischer, *op. cit.*, vol. 57, p. xvi.

Nach Aurifaber's erster Ausgabe, mit sorgfältiger Vergleichung sowohl der Stangwald'schen als der Selneccers' schen redaktion herausgegeben und erläutert von Karl Eduard Förstemann, und Heinrich Ernst Bindseil . . . . Berlin.

Four Volumes, 1844-1848.

22. *Martin Luthers Tischreden.* Den Deutschen Volke der Gegenwart angeeignet von Dr. R. L. B. Wolf. Leipzig, 1852. This is a selection from the Tischreden made by Wolff.[1]

23. *Dr. Martin Luthers Sämmtliche Werke.* Frankfurt a. M. and Erlangen. 1854. Dr. Mart. Luthers vermischte deutsche Schriften. Nach den ältesten Ausgaben kritisch und historisch bearbeitet von Dr. Johann Konrad Irmischer. II *Tischreden.* Vols. 57-62.

24. *Dr. Martin Luthers Sämmtliche Schriften* herausgegeben von Dr. Joh. Georg. Walch. Zweiundzwansigster Band. *Colloquia oder Tischreden.* St. Louis, Mo., Lutherscher Concordia-Verlag. 1887. *Dr. Martin Luthers Colloquia oder Tischreden.* Zum ersten Male berichtigt und erneuert durch übersetzung der beiden Hauptquellen der Tischreden aus der lateinischen Originalen, nämlich des Tagebuchs des Dr. Conrad Cordatus über Dr. M. Luther, 1537 und des Tagebuchs des M. Anton Lauterbach auf das Jahr, 1538.[2]

25. *Luthers Tischreden.* Schmidt. 1878. A small selection " für das Christlichen Haus."

26. *Kraft-Sprüche Dr. Martin Luthers.* Aus der Original Ausgabe seiner Tischreden von J. Aurifaber zusammen gestellt und mit erläuternden Anmerkungen versehen von A Reichenbach. Leipzig, 1883.

[1] Hartford Theological Seminary Library.
[2] Union Theological Seminary Library.

27. *Luthers Schriften* in Bd 15 of the series *Deutsche National Literature.* Ed. by E. Wolf. 1884-1892. A very small selection of the *Tischreden* at the end of this. 28. *Meyers Volksbücher. Luthers Tischreden.* Six small volumes, each dedicated to a separate subject. 1889-92.

Probably a large number of other editions of the same character as the last four—little selections for the edification of the pious Lutheran, or for the amusement of those interested in German history and literature—have been published. They are of so little importance that I have not thought it worth while to make an exhaustive search for them.

Latin Editors[1]

29. *Colloquia, meditationes, consolationes, consilia, judicia, sententiae, narrationes, responsa, facetiae D. Martini Lutheri, piae et sanctae memoriae, in mensa prandii et coenae, et in peregrinationibus observata et fideliter transscripta.* Francofurti ad Moenum. Rebenstock. 2 vols. 1571.[2]

[1] There is one little book which purports to be a Latin edition of the *Tischreden*, but it is not. I mean: "*Sylvula Sententiarum, Exemplorum, Facetiarum*, Partim ex Reverendi Viri, D. Martini Lutheri, ac Philippi Melanthonis cum privatis tum publicis relationibus; Partim ex aliorum veterum atq. recentium Doctorum monumentis observata & in Locos Communes ordine Alphabetico disposita. . . . . Per N. Ericeum. [Pictures of Luther and Melanchthon] Francofurti ad Moenum, per Petrum Fabricium & Sigismundum Feyerbend. 1566." This is a mere collection of odds and ends from writings of and about Luther; no proper Colloquia. It may be compared to the *Table Talk* of Dr. Samuel Johnson, collected from his writings and from Boswell.

[2] Rebenstock's name is not on the titlepage, but in the preface. The first volume was dated 1558 in all descriptions of this rare work, until Bindseil, in his *Colloquia*, preface, discovered the true date of both volumes to be 1571. The confusion arose from the fact that a picture was inserted on the first page, which bore the date (singularly enough) 1558; the Preface, however, was signed and dated 1571.

30. *D. Martini Lutheri Colloquia, meditationes, consolationes, iudiciae, sententiae, narrationes, responsa, facetiae.* E codice Bibliothecae Orphanotrophei Halensis cum perpetua collatione Editionis Rebenstockianae edita et prolegominis indicibusque instructa ab Henrico Ernesto Bindseil. 3 vols. 1863-1866. Lemgoviae et Detmoldiae.

Printed Editions of Sources

31. *M. Anton Lauterbachs Diaconi zu Wittenberg, Tagebuch auf das Jahr, 1538, die Hauptquelle der Tischreden Luthers.* Aus der Handschrift herausgegeben von Lic. theol. Johann Karl Seidemann Pastor zu Eschdorf. Dresden, 1872.

32. *Tagebuch über Dr. Martin. Luther geführet von Dr. Conrad Cordatus, 1537.* Zum ersten Male Herausgegeben von Dr. H. Wrampelmeyer . . . Halle . . . 1885.

33. *Luthers Tischreden aus den Jahren 1531 und 1532.* Nach den Aufzeichnungen von Joh. Schlaginhaufen. Von W. Preger. Leipzig, 1888.

34. *Analecta Lutherana et Melanthonia.* Von G. Lösche. Gotha 1892.

35. *Luthers Tischreden in der Mathesischen Sammlung.* Aus einer Handschrift der Leipziger Stadtbibliothek herausgegeben von Ernst Kroker . . . Leipzig, 1903.

This publication contains, besides 772 numbers from the Leipsig MS., 2 from Bavarus, 1 each from Cordatus B and Analecta, 6 from Memorabilia, and 65 from Serotina.

PART V.   TRANSLATIONS

English

1. *Dris. Martini Lutheri Colloquia Mensalia* or *Dr. Martin Luther's Divine Discourses at his Table*, which

in his Lifetime he held with divers Learned Men, such as were Philip Melanchthon, Casparus Cruciger, Justus Jonas, Paulus Eberus, Vitus Dietericus Johannes Bugenhagen, Johannes Forsterus, and Others.   Containing Questions and Answers Touching Religion and other main points of Doctrine; as also Many notable Histories, and all sorts of Learning, Comforts, Advices, Prophecies, Admonitions, Directions and Instructions, Collected first together by Dr. Antonius Lauterbach, And afterwards disposed into certain Commonplaces by John Aurifaber, D. D.   Translated from the High German into the English Tongue by Captain Henry Bell.   London: Printed by William Du-Gard, dwelling in Suffolk-lane, near London-stone, 1652.[1]

2. *The same*, 1791.   The title is the same down to Captain Henry Bell, then come the words: Second Edition. To which is prefixed, " The Life and Character of Dr. Martin Luther: by John Gottlieb Burckhardt, D. D., minister of the German Lutheran Congregation at the Savoy, in London.   London: Printed for the Proprietor, W Heptinstal, No. 3 Wood Street, Spa Fields, Clerkenwell. MDCCXCI.[2]

3. *Familiar Discourses of Martin Luther.*   Translated by Captain Bell and revised by J Kerby.   Lewes, 1818.[3]

4. *Choice Fragments from the Discourses of Luther.* London, 1832.[4]

5. *The Table Talk or Familiar Discourses of Martin*

---

[1] Copy at Union Seminary.   The titlepage is preceded by a full-length picture of Luther.

[2] The Lane Theological Seminary, of Cincinnati, Ohio, was kind enough to let me see its copy of this edition, which I have not found elsewhere.

[3] Catalogue of Brit. Museum.

[4] Lenox Library.

Luther.   Translated by William Hazlitt, Esq.   London, MDCCCXLVIII.

6. *The same* in *Bohn's Library,* with Luther's Life by Dr. Chalmers.   1857.[1]

7. *The same.*   1900.

8. *The same;* American Edition by Lutheran Publishing Co. of Philadelphia.[2]

9. *The Table-Talk of Doctor Martin Luther.*   IVth Centenary edition edited by T Fisher Unwin.   London, 1883.[1]

10. *Luther at Table.*   *Elegant Extracts from his Talk.*   W. H. Anderson, London, 1883.[1]

11. *Luther's Table Talk.*   Extracts selected by Dr. Macauley.   1883.[1]

12. Selections from the Table Talk of Martin Luther. Translated by Bell.   Cassell's *National Library,* Vol. 14, 1886.[1]

Tischreden may also be found in translation in the following volumes:

13. *Luther's Life written by himself,* arranged and translated by Lawson.   Edinburgh, 1832.

14. *Luther's Life by himself.*   Arranged by J Michelet, Translated by Wm Hazlitt.   1846.

15. The same translated by Smith.   New York, 1846.[3]

16. The *Prophecies of Luther concerning the Downfall of Rome.*   Collected by R. C. m. a.   London, 1664.[1]

17. Warner's *Library of the World's Best Literature.* Selection from Hazlitt.

18. *Words that shook the world, or Martin Luther his own biographer.*   New York, 1858.   By C Adams.[3]

---

[1] Catalogue of Brit. Museum.

[2] So they write me, but give no date.

[3] Astor Library.

French Translations

1. *Les Propos de Table de Martin Luther*, Révus sur les editions originales, et traduits pour la première fois en Français. Paris, 1844. By Gustave Brunet.

Some *Tischreden* are also translated into French in the following:

2. *Mémoires de Luther écrits par lui-même;* traduits et mis en ordre par M. Michelet . . . . Paris, 1835.

3. *The same* Bruxelles 1845.

4. Audin: *Histoire de la vie, des ouvrages et des doctrine de Luther.* 1839.

PART VI.   WORKS RELATING TO THE *TISCH-REDEN*

Most of the textual criticism of the *Tischreden* is to be found in the introductions to the various editions enumerated above.   The older editions are worth little, even Bindseil's Introductions to the fourth volume of the Förstemann-Bindseil edition of the German *Tischreden*, and to his edition of the Latin *Colloquia*, though showing more acumen and a greater grasp and critical ability than any of the preceding, are worth less than more recent work, because of the publication of so many of the sources, which has made the old collections comparatively valueless. Criticism of the texts of the sources began with Seidmann's Introduction to *Lauterbach's Tagebuch,* (1872), which is confined to a description of MSS. and their authors and possessors in such condensed form as to be little more than a series of exhaustive references.   The copious Introduction and notes of Wrampelmeyer (to *Cordatus Tagebuch,* 1885) hardly went outside the field of his own MS., though he added many parallels to this.   His judgment was warped by over-appreciation of his text.   Preger,

in his Introduction to *Schlaginhauffen's Notes* (1888) is
valuable for his researches on Dietrich and Schlaginhaufen's
notes. He aims to strike the happy mean " zwischen dem
Seidemann'schen zu wenig und dem Wrampelmeyer'schen
zu viel." Lösche, in the Introduction to his *Analecta Lutherana at Melanthonia* (1892), gave the most complete
account of MSS. up to that time published, though his interpretation of his own text as a copy of the Mathesian Collection turned out incorrect. He indulges in a somewhat
pretentious style, speaking of Luther and Melanchthon as
the " Reformatorische Dioscuri," and commenting severely
on the " niedriges niveau " shown by Melancthon's telling
stories in his class-room. By far the best thing that has
come out on the texts, up to date, both for amount of detailed work, and for a large grasp of critical principles, is
Kroker's Introduction to his edition of the *Mathesian Collection.* (1903).

The only piece of work on the texts of the *Collections* is
found in the article of W. Meyer aus Speyer: " Ueber Lauterbachs und Aurifabers Sammlungen d. Tischreden Luthers." *In Abhandlungen d. k. Gesellsch. d. Wissenschaften z. Göttingen. Phil-Hist. Kl.* Neue Folge Bd. 1. Nr. 2.
1897. He first established the relation of Lauterbach and
Aurifaber, proving that Lauterbach had made several redactions. He based his conclusions on an examination of the
MSS. which shows real German *Gründlichkeit.*

A considerable amount of periodical literature on the
texts might be cited, but it is either in the form of an-
nouncements of MSS. to be published (*e. g.,* H. E.
Bindseil: " Bemerkungen über die Deutschen und Lateinischen Tischreden Luthers," in *Theol. Stud u. Krit.,* 1866,
pp. 702-716), or of reviews of the same, which in any case
appeared in better form in the critical apparatus of the edition in question.

For light on contemporary events and the place of *Tischreden* in history: encyclopedias, works on the Reformation, lives of Luther, and Luther's works, must all be consulted. For particular points, such as the life of one of the *Tischgesellen*, A. Hauck's *Realencyclopädie für protestantische Theologie und Kirche*, 3d. ed. which is now appearing (last vol. XVII, 1906 to *Schutzheilige*), is indispensable. Somewhat less useful is the Catholic counterpart, the *Kirchenlexicon* in 12 vols. (completed in 1901). I have also used the *Allgemeine Deutsche Bibliographie*.

General Histories of the Reformation say little about the *Tischreden,* Lavisse and Rambaud (Vol. IV, *Renaisance et Reforme* 1894) gives a brief, and rather harsh appreciation of them.

The lives of Luther, on the other hand, make much of them. Köstlin (*Martin Luther,* second edition, 1883) gives a good account of them (vol. i, p. 774, vol. ii, p. 487 *et seq.*), and refers to them as an authority in almost every note. Thoroughly sympathetic with his subject, he feels the amiability of Luther's domestic life, though he, like the other writers on the subject, thinks he must excuse the faults of taste. Hausrath, *Luthers Leben* (new ed., 1905) must also be mentioned. Lindsay in his small but excellent work, *Luther and the German Reformation,* 1903, speaks appreciatively of the *Tischreden* (p. 293). Döllinger, *Die Reformation, ihre innere Entwickelung* (1853-1854, 3 vols.), and Denifle, *Luther und Lutherthum,* (2 vols., 1904, 1905), attack the *Tischreden* from the other standpoint, finding in them a rich source of damaging material. Seckendorf, *Historie d. Lutherthums* (German ed., 1714), gives some early reference which throw light on occasional points.

Luther's *Works* are of course the most valuable contemporary source in explaining allusions and clearing up obscurities. The splendid edition coming out now at *Weimar* (29 vols., published 1883-1904) is the best. Walch, *Sämtliche* Werke 24 vols., 1740-1753) is good. Luther's Letters are the source most closely related to the *Tischreden*. De Wette, *Luthers Briefe* (6 vols., 1825-56), covers his whole life. Ender's *Luthers Briefwechsel* now appearing, is fuller (Vol. X. to July, 1536, 1903).

For special purposes the following works on Luther's Life or Works have been referred to:

Lingke: *Merkwürdige Reisegeschichte Luther's*, 1769.

F. S. Keil: *Merkwürdige Lebensumstände Luther's*, 1764.

Kolde: *Analecta Lutherana*, 1883. This is a collection of miscellaneous contemporary sources.

Bretschneider: *Corpus Reformatorum*, vol. 1-28, Melanchthon. 1834-1860.

Kawerau: *Briefwechsel d. J. Jonas*. 2 vols, 1884-5, vol. 17 of *Geschichtsquellen d. Provinz Sachsen*.

Lösche: *Johannes Mathesius. Ein Lebens und Sittenbild aus der Reformationzeit*. 2 Bd. Gotha, 1905.

Lösche: *G. Mathesius' Ausgewählte Werke*. 4 Bd. *New Ed. Prag.*, 1904. The principle contents of this work is the " Luther Histories " which we have spoken of as a source of the *Tischreden* also.

Buchwald: *Mathesius' Predigten über Luthers Leben*, 1904, publishes them again.

Rockwell, W. W.: *Die Doppelehe des Landgrafen Philipp von Hessen*. 1904.

Little is to be found on the literary aspect of the *Tischreden*. The Histories of German Literature (Vilmar, Scherer, Francke) ignore them. Most of the editors by way of literary appreciation indulge in a few lugubrious remarks on the coarseness to be found in them. Walch (Einl. to Bd. xxii, see *supra*) gives a short analysis of their contents. Special aspects of the *Tischreden* are spoken of in the following:

Möller & Stricker: *Benignissimo Facultatis Philosophicae indultu, auctoritatem scripti, sub titulo D. Lutheri Colloquiorum Mensalium Editi, considerabunt.* 1693. This is an impossible attempt to defend the Table Talk by proving it a forgery.

Eberhard, J. E.: *Schediasma Historicum de B. D. Lutheri Colloquiis Mensalibus,* 1698, (M DC XCIIX). This tiny quaint old monograph I picked up at a second-hand bookstore. It is very eloquent and very inane.

Zincgref, J. W.: *Teutsche scharfsinnige kluge Apophthegmata,* 1628, gives a number of little stories and proverbs attributed to Luther, most of which are apocryphal.

Xanthippus: "Gute alte deutsche Sprüche." Three articles in *Preussischen Jahrbücher,* vol. 85. (July to September, 1896.) Pp. 149, 344, 503. This gives an interesting and accurate view of the influence of the *Tischreden* on German proverbial speech.

Chasle, Philarète: "La Renaissance Sensuelle; Luther, Rabelais, Skelton, Folengo," in *Revue des Deux Mondes,* Mar., 1842. This once celebrated writer sees in Luther the apostle of the movement against asceticism which he thinks preceded the Reformation.

Hereford, C. H.: *Studies in the Literary Relations of England and Germany in the 16th Century.* 1886. This author, although he says in his Preface "for us Luther is solely the author of *Ein Feste Burg,*" throws some light on allusions in the *Tischreden* to contemporary German literature, as for example in his short treatment of "Grobianus and Grobianism." (Pp. 379, 380. *Cf.,* Wrampelmeyer, no. 1738.)

Robinson, J. H.: "*The Study of the Lutheran Revolt.*" *Am. Hist. Rev.,* Jan., 1903. A critical review of recent literature on the Protestant Revolt.

Rolffs, E.: "Luthers Humor ein Stuck seiner Religion." Preussische Jahrbücher 1904, vol. 155. Pp. 468-488. Treats this side of Luther's style in an agreeable and popular manner.

Weiss, J.: *Luthers Einfluss auf die deutsche Literatur*. This author says nothing about the *Tischreden*, but is worth mentioning for his general treatment of the subject.

Schmidt, E.: "Faust und Luther." In *König. preus. Akademie der Wissenschaften zu Berlin Sitzungsberichte*, July, 1896. P. 567.

Brunet, G.: Introduction to the *Propos de Table*, gives a bright, though superficial appreciation of the subject.

The following may be mentioned as important linguistic helps in reading Luther's *Tischreden*:

Du Cange: *Glossarium mediae et infimae Latinitatis*.

Grimm: *Deutsches Wörterbuch*. Vols. I-X (to *sprechen*, 1905).

Dietz: *Luther Wörterbuch*. Vol. I, A-H. 1870.

Schmeller: *Bayrischer Wörterbuch*, bearbeitet von G. K. Fromman, München, 1877. This is the best of the dictionaries for dialectical peculiarities which often appear in Luther's speech. It is phonetically arranged, the b's and p's coming together, for example, a sensible plan as they are so freely interchangeable.

Opitz, K. E.: *Luthers Sprache*. Ein Beitrag zur geschichte des Neuhochdeutschen. 1869.

No complete bibliography of any branch of the literature can be found. For the MSS., the Introductions to Kroker, and Lösche's *Analecta,* and the article of Meyer before mentioned, supplement each other. For the editions, the lists in the Introductions of the editions of Irmischer, Walch and Förstemann-Bindseil are good for the time pre-

ceding their issue, but are not complete. One may also
consult :

British Museum Catalogue; Section on Luther printed
separately 1894.
Fabritius: Centifolium Lutheranum.[1]
Zuchold: Bibliotheca Theologica Vol. ii.
Hinrich's Catalogues 1750 to date.
Köstlin op. cit., vol. ii., pp. 723-733.
Real-Encyclopädie. Article " Luther," more recent.

[1] I have not seen this, but it is continually referred to by Irmischer
and Walch, being apparently their chief source.

VITA

THE author of this dissertation, Preserved Smith, was born at Cincinnati, Ohio, on July 22, 1880. He graduated from Amherst College in the class of 1901, with the degree of A. B., being awarded the Roswell Hitchcock Fellowship in History on completing his course. The years 1901–1903 and 1906-1907, respectively, he spent in study at Columbia University, under the Faculty of Political Science pursuing courses primarily in the department of history. In 1902 he obtained the degree of Master of Arts, and in the following year was awarded the Schiff Fellowship. He taught in the Department of Government at Williams College for the two years 1904–1906.